THE POLICE STAFF COLLEGE
BRAMSHILL HOUSE
BRAMSHILL
HOOK, HAMPSHIRE
RG27 0JW

THE
EFFECTIVE
DELIVERY
OF
TRAINING
USING NLP

*A HANDBOOK OF TOOLS, TECHNIQUES
AND PRACTICAL EXERCISES*

TED GARRATT

**KOGAN
PAGE**

London • Stirling (USA)

First published in 1997

Kogan Page Limited
120 Pentonville Road
London N1 9JN
and
22883 Quicksilver Drive
Stirling, VA 20166, USA

British Library Cataloguing in Publication Data

A CIP record for this book is available from the British Library.

ISBN 0 7494 2142 8 hardback

Typeset by JS Typesetting, Wellingborough, Northants
Printed and bound in Great Britain by Clays Ltd St Ives plc

CONTENTS

Preface   vii

Introduction   **1**
How to use this book   1
Background to NLP   2
NLP and training   6

Chapter 1. Creating The Right Environment   **11**
1.1   Styles of training   11
1.2   Creating rapport   15
1.3   Creating and maintaining high expectations   21
1.4   Creating rituals and engaging emotions   25
1.5   Using exercise bursts to create energy   27
1.6   Acknowledging different learner styles   29

Chapter 2. Creating An Effective Personal State   **33**
2.1   Maintaining a positive personal state   33
2.2   Creating personal flexibility   36
2.3   Being a learning trainer   38
2.4   Behaviour modelling and strategies   40
2.5   Setting own personal outcomes   44
2.6   Using anchors   45
2.7   Using perceptual positions   48
2.8   Using a variety of training techniques   51
2.9   Using context as well as content clues   51
2.10 Using a big picture/little picture technique   54
2.11 Understanding brain hemisphere functions   55
2.12 Using calibration   60
2.13 Using congruence   62
2.14 Using association/disassociation   62

Chapter 3. Getting The Message Across   **67**
  3.1   Using language patterns   67
  3.2   Using metaphors   77
  3.3   Using reframing   82
  3.4   Using backtracking   85
  3.5   Using sleight of mouth   87
  3.6   Using quotes   90
  3.7   Using embedded commands   91
  3.8   Using relevancy challenges   93
  3.9   Gathering information   94
  3.10 Communicating clearly and effectively   97
  3.11 Using pre-suppositions   98
  3.12 Using effective questions   99
  3.13 Using eye accessing clues   100

Chapter 4. Being Flexible To Meet The Needs   **105**
  4.1   Getting participants to set own goals   105
  4.2   Pacing and leading a group   108
  4.3   Using non-verbal communication   112
  4.4   Creating group dynamics   117
  4.5   Changing learner states   120
  4.6   Using humour   122
  4.7   Switching roles and styles   125
  4.8   Being aware of invisibles (values, beliefs, identity) 127
  4.9   Creating reference experiences   129
  4.10 Creating new learning patterns   132
  4.11 Noticing behavioural changes   136
  4.12 Using effective feedback   138
  4.13 Unsticking people   146
  4.14 Using reverse tests   148
  4.15 Maintaining involvement   151
  4.16 Instructing people   152
  4.17 Creating positive beliefs   153
  4.18 Using accelerated learning   155
  4.19 Using timelines   162
  4.20 Using future pacing   166
  4.21 Using Meta Programs   167
  4.22 Tasking people   184
  4.23 Using chunking   185
  4.24 Using sub-modalities   186
  4.25 Using memory techniques   194
  4.26 Using present state – desired state   204
  4.27 Using edits   205
  4.28 Using the new behaviour generator   208
  4.29 Using internal dialogue   209

Chapter 5. Confirming The Learning   **213**
    5.1   Revising objectives   213
    5.2   Agreeing action plans   214
    5.3   Using checklists   215
    5.4   Effective endings   216
    5.5   Post-course self-evaluation   217
    5.6   Learning for next time   218

Glossary of Terms   219
Bibliography   223
Index   227

PREFACE

'I have learned silence from the talkative, toleration from the intolerant and kindness from the unkind; yet strange I am ungrateful to those teachers.'
Kahlil Gibran

Why write a book about NLP and training? This thought has recurred to me ever since someone initially suggested the idea. If you are in the field of NLP there are large numbers of books already, with more arriving all the time, and books on training are not in short supply either.

It is the combination of the two, NLP and training, that provided the motivation, along with a third point, *delivery* of training. The most important part of NLP, for me, is its practicality. Delivery of training is also, or should be, about what works, so they do all fit together.

This is also because of how I became aware of and involved in NLP in the first place. In 1991, I had run my own Human Resource (HR) consultancy for seven years and worked in HR and training for a previous ten years. During this time I felt that I had exposure to, or actively used, pretty well every management model and theory. Most of them had something to offer, but not always enough.

In addition, as someone who ran training courses for a living, I found that some skills, techniques and exercises worked better than others. Or something that worked well in one set of circumstances failed totally in another. I was intrigued as to how this could be, perhaps it was just the famous catch-all 'human nature'. I decided to try to get behind the skills, techniques and exercises to find out what made these things happen. Almost without exception I came up against NLP, in some form or other.

My initial reaction was 'What on earth is this thing called NLP?' (not an unusual reaction). The title itself seemed to be overly complex and off putting, in fact it sounded scary and mysterious, so I decided to find out more.

Like most people I read a book and like most people it was *Frogs Into Princes* by Richard Bandler and John Grinder. I understood some of it, didn't understand a lot more, but my curiosity was aroused. At the time I thought I was the only person on the planet following this route. So I was amazed when I signed up for practitioner training to find 60 other spirits in the same room, each on their own quest.

The training I received at practitioner and master practitioner was the most useful, fun and interesting training I had ever undertaken. However, with it came a shock. I approached the training to acquire skills to use on other people, it never occurred to me that I would be able to 'do it to myself'. In fact, if I had, I might not have attended, but right from the first weekend the uses of NLP to develop, grow and change myself were made apparent. Not bad in two days of training. In addition, I was fascinated by the other delegates. Some were from business but many were not. There were therapists of every description, people looking for a change of direction, in general people who were doing different things to me. This proved to be a major plus in all the NLP trainings I undertook.

I started my NLP training in 1992 and like all NLP-ers it is still going on (most NLP-ers require a 'fix' at least biannually). Every time there is new material, thoughts, ideas, skills and techniques; in fact, in many ways the pace is accelerating in terms of what is available in all these areas.

In addition, I have had nearly five years to incorporate NLP into my trainings. I don't run NLP courses, I run courses in lots of subjects and include the key NLP processes wherever they are appropriate, often without NLP ever being mentioned. For example, in running a coaching course for a group of middle managers in a chemical business, they don't want to know about Meta Programs, but they do want to know about why the people they are coaching do what they do, and how to respond to it.

Another aspect in deciding to write this book was watching other trainers work. Because NLP is based on what works, good trainers, even if they have never heard of NLP, follow its principles and apply its skills. It has been a joy to watch highly skilled people help delegates at courses and conferences and to recognize, acknowledge and model them. Good trainers already do lots of these things, but may not know they are doing them, or how they are doing them, or why they work. They apply the skills and techniques pragmatically, purposefully, positively, with elegance, respect and integrity, because they work.

INTRODUCTION

HOW TO USE THIS BOOK

> 'The mystery of life is not a problem to be solved.
> It is a reality to be experienced.'
> Van der Leeuw

NLP has its own language and jargon (more so than many other fields). In writing a book it is tempting to play with the language or make up new, more user-friendly, words. But within NLP this is what they are called, so I have stuck with them. It is not the jargon that matters, it is about what works and creating a more flexible range of skills.

The book is about the delivery of training. This is not to ignore the importance of preparation, training design, analysing needs, etc. The NLP processes can be applied to all these areas. What this book is for is to give trainers things to use and do – lots of them. Therefore, the lists and exercises are designed to be used easily rather than read in the conventional way.

The basic structure is three-stage.

1. Each section has an overview of the topic.
2. The discussion is followed by a series of exercises.
3. Key points are summarized at the end.

The exercises do repeat and overlap. This is deliberate and as it should be. None of the NLP processes stand alone. Trainers should be able not only to follow the exercises in the book, but cross-fertilize many of them from topic to topic, or even make up their own.

If some of the exercises are not felt to be appropriate, go to the Bibliography, buy a book and find some more. One thing that NLP has in abundance is a huge range of exercises to assist achievement of change. Also be prepared to play. There is a danger in trying to capture things in print of making them appear lifeless, esoteric, even scary. NLP is about what works, it is fun and practical, go play with it.

Remember it is not necessary to become trained in NLP (although that would be a preferred first step), so you do not need to be an expert. However, being open, curious and willing to try something new helps enormously.

Finally, some guidelines to get the most from this book:

- be curious;
- test what works;
- use it in the real world (not just in your head);
- look for what works, not what doesn't;
- discuss and practise with other people;
- do an NLP training;
- create some positive outcomes;
- read other books.

BACKGROUND TO NLP

> *'They know enough who know how to learn.'*
> Henry Adams

So what is this thing called NLP?

A source of confusions for many people is that a number of definitions are used. These range from:

'The study of the structure of subjective experience.'

through 'An attitude that leaves behind a trail of techniques.'

to 'It's what works.'

My favourite is 'The difference that makes the difference'. Inevitably, it is all these things and many more. In many ways there is nothing new in NLP. What it does provide is an explanation of why some things work or happen. Therefore, it is a discovery, not an invention. Like language it encodes human behaviour and experience. As an output from this comes the myriad of techniques.

The co-developers of NLP were two Americans. Richard Bandler was a mathematician and a student of psychology, and John Grinder a linguist. At the suggestion of Gregory Bateson, the eminent anthropologist, they decided to analyse some of the foremost communicators and therapists in the world to find out what they were doing, how they were doing it, and why it worked. In particular they studied Milton Ericson, Fritz Perls and Virginia Satir, all leaders in their field.

The aspects that Bandler and Grinder focused on were what worked. They spent an enormous amount of time with the three models, analysing every aspect of what they did, most of it unconsciously (the therapists that is!) The patterns that emerged were tested and worked. These were based on certain beliefs, unconscious verbal and non-verbal strategies, ways of thinking, and the way that they were applied became a model for excellence.

To many people this was a completely new concept, that excellence could be analysed, modelled and passed on to others. The applications of this concept in sport, business, therapy and other walks of life have provided ongoing information and patterns, which have been added in as the years have gone by.

So why Neuro Linguistic Programming? Part of the answer is because of the backgrounds of the originators. In addition each part of the title carries a particular relevance.

Neuro: how the brain process actually works. Based on how people take experience and illustrate physiologically.

Linguistic: the actual way these experiences are represented by the use of language.

Programming: the specific patterns and programmes of behaviour and thought to produce a consistent and/or specific result.

In studying NLP these three processes actually become explicit.

Having carried out the modelling part of what produced excellent results, the next stage was to share the results, test them in as many situations as possible and add to the original work. This is still happening today, resulting in a growing set of tools that anyone can use. In addition, it allows people to develop their own level of competence and excellence, hence its growing use in so many diverse areas of human activity.

Operating principles

Anyone who attends an NLP training will start with the operating principles. At first glance they can look simplistic, obvious and straight-forward (or just wrong).

At a conference I heard Stephen Covey, the well-known management guru, remark that 'the best form of simplicity emerges on the far side of complexity'. These principles takes some living up to, and the longer I have worked with them the deeper and more meaningful they have become.

The map is not the territory
Everyone has their own map, eg beliefs and values regarding the world. In order to make sense of the world we put experience into our map, we then do things from that map.

You cannot not communicate
Everything we do (or don't do) may carry some meaning and significance to someone else.

The meaning of your communication is the response you get
If the response is different from your intention, that's the way it is. How many times at work (or at home) have we said 'I thought you knew what I meant'? Well they *did* think they knew what we meant. We just didn't get our meaning across effectively.

There is no failure only feedback
If we look for failure, guess what, we will find it. This doesn't mean that everything will always work for us, or that we need to hype ourselves up to see the good in everything. Seeing everything as feedback enables us to make more appropriate choices next time.

Everyone makes the best choice available to them at the time
In my early days in NLP this was the one operating principle I had most trouble with. I believed that people could be 'wrong' or 'right' (often based on my rather limited map of the world). Again this doesn't mean we condone all our own behaviour, but it does mean we should stop beating ourselves up unnecessarily. NLP can help develop a more flexible range of choice.

One of the wonderful ways this operating principle helps us is in our relationship with others, either at work or outside. Rather than label or blame them, our role becomes to help them have more choices for next time (but remember *they* will make their choices, which may not be the same as ours).

People already have all the resources they need
This is a real challenge for many people who believe that other people (and occasionally themselves) are difficult, and laden down with problems that should be sorted out, ie that in some way they are 'broken' and need fixing. This is a big issue for a trainer who can be perceived as (and believe themselves to be) a 'fixer' or guru who can solve all their problems at a stroke. The role of the trainer is to help them find their own best way to achieve the end result, not to tell them they are wrong or in need of external assistance and provide the trainer's own solutions.

Those with the greatest flexibility control the situation
This is based on Ashby's Law of Requisite Variety. If what we are doing isn't working, just doing more of it (but louder) almost certainly won't work either.

If what you are doing isn't working, do something different
Throughout this book this is a constant message. It doesn't mean flailing around from technique to technique, but rather always bearing the positive outcome in mind, and be looking to try anything in order to achieve it.

Some of these principles may appear to be unrealistic or difficult, some people would say they may not be the truth. But try acting as if they were and see what this does to your model of the world and how it develops a richer view of both yourself and other people.

Representation systems

One other key aspect when understanding NLP is the role that representation systems play. Human beings take in information through all their five senses, which NLP has coded as:

V	Visual	Pictures
A	Auditory	Words
K	Kinesthetic	Feeling, sensations, emotions
O	Olfactory	Smell
G	Gustatory	Taste

Throughout NLP literature reference is made to these codings; from eye accessing cues, through language patterns to behaviour modelling and strategies.

The preference that learners will have in using their representation systems will be a significant factor in helping them find the best ways to learn. Also to retain the information and skills so that effective and ongoing change will occur. It also is of great interest and curiosity to the learner who almost certainly will not have been, at least consciously, aware of their preferences before. For many it will explain why some types of training have worked and some haven't. It also allows them to create more effective strategies for the future.

Equally this can also apply to the trainers themselves. The greater awareness they have, both as a learner and a trainer, the more flexible and effective they can become.

NLP AND TRAINING

'It is better to know some of the questions than all of the answers.'
James Thurber

As I said in the Preface, what lead me to NLP was that every time I tried to get behind something that worked, both on a training course, and outside it, I kept coming up against NLP in some form or other. Therefore, over a period of time I started to do things deliberately, much of which I had done all along, but unconsciously. This actually can be a very strange step, as making something explicit can somehow seem to make it obvious to everyone or even manipulative. Suddenly finding out why something works can raise all sorts of issues.

On the point of it being obvious, there was no need for concern. Learners didn't notice that I was matching their language patterns or finding out how they set goals by asking Meta Program type questions. What they did notice was that it helped, worked, and often resulted in a breakthrough for the learner (thus creating a reference experience for them).

Regarding the second concern, it can only be manipulative if it was being done for my end rather than theirs, which of course would not work as my intention would become obvious. Clarifying their outcomes and working inside the operating principles of NLP ensures that the integrity of all parties is maintained.

How training and NLP fit together

NLP is about what people do, how they do it and why they do it. It is about developing skills and techniques, modelling and creating excellence, having positive outcomes, working with integrity and in harmony with people and much more. I would argue that training is about the same things.

Applications of NLP in the field of training are:

- designing training programmes;
- finding out how people learn (and why);
- developing strategies for success;
- modelling these strategies based upon success and what works, then taking it further;
- helping learners find their own 'best way';
- giving learners practical tools;
- allowing learners to experiment;
- focusing on outcomes;
- developing the trainer's skills;

- improving the delivery of training;
- helping the trainer be a role-model;
- making training even more fun, interesting and useful;
- helping deal with limiting beliefs about learning (this can apply to the trainer as well);
- creating reference experiences for people;
- evaluating training;
- moving training from the training room onward into the 'real' world (based upon the individual learners particular map of the world).

Specific applications in training programmes

Some aspect of NLP will be evident and useful in every aspect of training. From creating rapport, through to establishing outcomes, to modelling strategies for success. Specific courses that it can be used for include:

- any form of interviewing;
- team building;
- coaching;
- mentoring;
- negotiating;
- selling;
- change management;
- risk management;
- creating corporate culture;
- people skills;
- presentations;
- inter-personal skills;
- effective meetings;
- leadership;
- motivation;
- influencing and persuading;
- outdoor training programmes.

CREATING THE RIGHT ENVIRONMENT

1

CREATING THE RIGHT ENVIRONMENT

'There is one thing to be said about ignorance, it certainly causes lots of arguments.'
Anon

Many trainers make the mistake of thinking that once they have done the groundwork, analysed the need, got themselves ready and created effective training programmes, all they have to do is deliver them. Those that carry this through into the training environment almost inevitably lose all the benefits of having carried out the first steps properly.

Equally, effective delivery of training is the part of the process that the audience will focus on, discuss and carry away with them as their prime memory of the whole event. Many trainers concentrate totally on their understanding of the subject matter, having the right quality of visual aids and handouts available, and ensuring that all the breaks are properly planned. All of these factors are absolutely vital, *but* the depth and strength of the message and content will be lost if the quality of the trainer is not of the same high standard. Therefore, this chapter is about putting the right building blocks in place.

1.1 STYLES OF TRAINING

There are many models and theories on how people learn, some of the most popular being Honey and Mumford's Learning Styles Questionnaire (LSQ), which gives feedback on whether the learner prefers to use an Activist, Pragmatist, Theorist or Reflector style. Another well-known example is the Learning Styles Inventory (Kolb, 1976), which breaks down responses into Accommodator, Diverger, Converger and Assimilator. Both of these are used extensively and include useful feedback and suggested action steps to be followed in order to develop a different profile. Most trainers would be familiar with these, or other inventories, and feel quite comfortable in using them in establishing training programmes (and to deliver effective training).

Less information is available on analysing trainer styles and some that is used can be contradictory. The long-running debate between the behaviourist style – which emphasizes control, shaping, prompting and reinforcing – and the humanist – which focuses on freedom, spontaneity, learner-centring, individuality and feelings – still goes on in some quarters.

The key point is that some trainers do not evidence flexibility in their style, but merely rely predominantly on the one they have always used, or have found to be the most successful. Therefore, irrespective of the needs of the learners they are given a dose of the training style that the trainer believes is best for them. Interestingly, the more under pressure trainers find themselves, the more likely it is that they will carry on with the style that is causing the problem in the first place.

In 1986 Wheeler and Marshall developed an instrument known as the Trainer Type Inventory which is based on Kolb's (1976) work on learning-style preferences. They break down trainer styles into *listener, director, interpreter* and *coach.*

Each style is differentiated by the way in which the content is presented and the nature of the relationship between trainer and trainee. The following are the primary characteristics for each training style.

Listener

- Allows free expression of learner needs.
- Highly aware of individuals.
- Training based on the here and now.
- Highly sensitive to non-verbals.
- Strong on empathy.
- Listens to all.
- Comfortable with all forms of expression.
- Open with own feelings and emotions.
- Prefers learners to be self-directed.
- Appears relaxed and at ease.
- 'Goes with the flow.'

Director

- Participation controlled by the trainer.
- Training based on 'how' and 'why'.
- Likes to take charge.
- Decides on what will be learnt.
- Well organized.
- Uses detailed training programmes.

- Has back up plans.
- Sticks to topics and timetable.
- Prefers to lecture.
- Self-confident.
- Uses objective criteria to evaluate.

Interpreter

- Wants learners to memorize things.
- Training based on 'there' and 'then'.
- Uses information based on objective data.
- Integrates theory and events by connecting the past to the present.
- Uses case studies.
- Likes to generalize and prefers independent thought.
- Prefers learners to understand all the facts and relevant information.
- Keeps a little separate.
- Shares ideas not feelings.
- Prefers the intellectual process.

Coach

- Prefers learners to be active.
- Wants learners to evaluate own progress.
- Training based on the 'what' and 'how'.
- Wants learners to experiment.
- Uses learners as a resource.
- Uses the strengths of the group.
- Visibly in charge.
- Uses real-life examples.
- Helps people express their knowledge.
- Acts as facilitator.

Also occasionally referred to is the Training Style Inventory developed in 1979 by Brostrom, which categorized four styles of training.

Behaviourist

- Believes that new behaviours can be caused and shaped with well-designed structures around the learner.
- Likes a supportive style.
- Tends to be clear, precise and deliberate.
- Prefers low risk.
- Uses careful preparation.
- Develops trust.
- Can create dependence.

Structuralist

- Believes the mind is like a computer and the trainer is the programmer.
- Uses lots of data and information.
- Uses a directive style.
- Well organized.
- Is an 'expert'.
- Well rehearsed.
- Focused on structure rather than results.

Functionalist

- Believes that people learn best by doing and will do best at what they want to do, and will learn what is practical.
- Bases judgements on performance 'on the job'.
- Likes a hands-on approach.
- Develops an assertive style.
- Likes to challenge learners.
- Acts as a coach.
- Gives opportunity and recognition.
- Believes that the ends justify the means.

Humanist

- Believes that learning is a self-directed discovery, that people are natural learners and will develop if nothing inhibits their progress.
- Likes learners to become better human beings.
- Creates space and freedom.
- Tends to be reflective.
- Focuses on relationships.
- Acts as a counsellor.
- Sensitive and responsive.
- Can appear vague, fuzzy and unprepared.

Michael Grinder, in *Righting the Educational Conveyor Belt*, offers the following NLP breakdown of trainer styles *when they are in instructing mode.*

Visual
Talks fast, uses visual aids, likes to cover lots of content, considers forms important (grammar, spelling, heading), believes in visual feedback, is due-date oriented.

Auditory
Speaks rhythmically, likes class discussion, likes to talk a lot, paraphrases learner comments and questions, disciplines by using stock repeated phrases and expressions, is easily moved from main topic – tells lots of war stories, uses a running commentary.

Kinesthetic
Talks slower, uses lots of handouts, uses lots of role play, simulations, likes concepts, likes demonstrations to evaluate, gets learners to do things, gets people working together.

During the next few years, as training evolves even more rapidly than at present, it is likely that much more work will be carried out regarding trainer styles and their impact on assisting effective learning.

STYLES OF TRAINING: EXERCISES

1. Analyse own training style and be aware of key strengths and weaknesses.
2. Analyse visual, auditory and kinesthetic preferences and be aware of key strengths and weaknesses.
3. Practise switching styles to create flexibility and match the needs of learners.
4. Watch other trainers to gauge their preferences and impact.
5. Use relevant NLP techniques to analyse what does and doesn't work, eg behaviour modelling/strategies.

STYLES OF TRAINING: KEY POINTS

☐ Be aware of your trainer style and its impact.
☐ Avoid becoming over dependent on one style, particularly when under pressure.
☐ Match the most effective style to materials.
☐ Work at developing greater flexibility in your trainer style.
☐ Watch other trainers and analyse how they do it.
☐ Use all the available NLP techniques to help achieve maximum effectiveness for both self and others.

1.2 CREATING RAPPORT

Of all the basic skills used within the trainer/trainee relationship rapport is the foundation for all the others. People are often aware of the importance of rapport on a one-to-one basis, or even within more structured formats, eg management meetings, but in a training context there is often group rapport taking place which the trainer is either unaware of, or excluded from. One reason for this is that trainers believe it to be too difficult to achieve with large groups and rely on their knowledge and/or materials to get them through.

Key skills of creating rapport

- Making a positive start.
- Fine-tuning to physiology and posture.
- Using varied voice tonalities.
- Recognizing learner language patterns.
- Using appropriate language patterns yourself.
- Observing breathing patterns.
- Using matching, cross-over matching and leading techniques.
- Recognizing when you are in or out of rapport.
- Using anchors.

Making a positive start

This applies whether it's the first or 101st time you have met and worked with the group. Greet people individually either informally with a smile or more formally with a handshake. Be warm and sincere and show that you are genuinely interested in being there with them at that time. One trainer, seen recently on a three day programme, actually started by saying that he believed that this place and the specific training about to be given were the single most important things in his life, at that precise moment. Over the next three days by the way he conducted himself and the quality of the training he carried out he was able to demonstrate to all 130 people in the audience that he actually meant it.

Other key aspects of making a positive start are:

- Give a brief but focused self-introduction.
- Use non-verbal ways of getting attention, these include:
  - use music;
  - get eye contact;
  - move around purposefully;
  - use appropriate gestures;
  - stand up straight;
  - stand in designated spot (see anchoring);
  - hold an unusual object;
  - use different lighting;
  - put energy into your voice;
  - consider using a question;
  - consider using a command;
  - state your name clearly;
  - use positive language.

CREATING RAPPORT: CASE STUDY

On a recent training course a small group of people, who knew each other well, became an obvious clique, which caused some resentment among other people on the course.

Their body posture was slumped and their language patterns predominantly kinesthetic except on an occasion when they became more enthusiastic about a topic when more visual and auditory words were used.

In talking to them over a break, rapport was achieved by matching body movements and language patterns. This was followed by then using more expansive gestures and visual and auditory words to lead them into a more positive state. This state was then anchored by a combination of voice tone, physiology and language and the whole dynamic of the course was changed. The clique actually split up and joined in with other course members.

Subsequently it was shown that they had been forced to attend and felt that it might not be relevant to their needs.

Fine-tuning to physiology and posture

It is important that you are open enough to pick up on the small signals that people in training will give out. Equally it is vital that you are in command of your own personal state and its impact on them.

Key actions are:

- Smile.
- Look for individual signals from trainees.
- Start to create rapport with key individuals.
- Start to create breathing patterns in trainees by use of humour and attention-getters.
- Match breathing patterns by watching shoulders.
- Pick up on gestures, eg tapping, fiddling, rocking to and fro, then match using a range of your own gestures.
- Be aware of posture and match it.
- Watch for and match facial expressions.
- Watch for evidence of being in rapport.

Using varied voice tonalities

As part of creating rapport, voice tonalities of the first people to speak, who may well be the official or unofficial leaders, can be very revealing. Also picking up later on in the training when voice tonalities start to change.

Key areas to be aware of are:

- Listen for volume levels.
- Listen to the pace, tempo and rate of speaking.
- Pick up on tonality, emphasis and pauses.

Recognizing learner language patterns

The types of words that trainees use, particularly at certain moments or about certain topics, will be very revealing of how they are processing the information and responding to it. (See 3.1 Using language patterns, page 67.) Specific areas to be aware of are:

- Words will reveal whether the trainee is processing information in a visual, auditory or kinesthetic way.
- Pick up on specific use of language and match it.
- Use appropriate metaphors (see 3.2 Using metaphors, page 77) ie match their background/roles.

Using appropriate language patterns yourself

As well as being aware of, and responding to the trainees' language patterns it is essential that trainers are equally aware of their own. If they have a tendency toward visual language and are working with a group of engineers or accountants who may be more auditory, it will actually create a lack of rapport, possibly without even realizing what is causing the problem (see 3.1 Using language patterns, page 67).

Observing breathing patterns

Arguably the single most effective way to create rapport is to observe and match breathing patterns. This should also blend in with all the other ways of creating rapport as when people are being visual they tend to breathe from the upper chest, when being auditory from the central chest and when into feelings from the lower chest and abdomen. It is also possible to create group breathing patterns by using humour and attention-getters to deliberately grab and focus the group's attention.

Another key skill is the ability to control and utilize your own breathing rate to create total self-control as well as create rapport with others.

Using matching, cross-over matching and leading techniques

Matching is the ability to create a shared common experience with other people. This is achieved by using your own observational skills to notice all the factors that have been mentioned so far (this skill is called calibration in NLP), then matching them to create rapport.

There is a fundamental difference between matching and mimicking and many people make the mistake of merely aping the person or group and actually breaking rapport. Matching is a much more subtle process than just folding your arms when someone else does, it requires lots of concentration on all the areas covered in this section to date, and includes blink rates, skin colour changes as well.

Another aspect of matching is known as cross-over matching. This involves picking up a signal, eg a tapping foot, from someone else and matching it by, for example, drumming your fingers. This is just as powerful as the more normal matching but operates at a much more subtle level.

The way to confirm that matching or cross-over matching has taken place is to lead. This means that *having achieved rapport*, you change a gesture or movement, speed up or slow down your voice, smile, or any other aspect of the clues covered above, and the other person/group follow your change and do it for themselves (see 4.2 Pacing and leading a group, page 108).

Recognizing when you are in or out of rapport

This requires constant vigilance in the group as well as very good self-awareness. It is very easy as a trainer to become totally self-preoccupied and miss all of the signals. Having one's attention turned outwards and inwards at the same time requires practice but can be achieved.

Using anchors

Establishing anchors at the beginning and early stages of training will help establish rapport from the beginning and they will also be available throughout the rest of the training.

Anchors (see 2.6 Using anchors, page 45) are best described as a process by which we make associations between experiences, eg useful – red traffic light and stopping; pleasurable – the smell of food and happy memories; accidental – having a police car overtake you and feeling apprehensive.

Anchors can be deliberately put in place by trainers and utilized wherever appropriate. This allows the learner to purposefully associate a specific and useful reaction to any stimulus they choose, eg feeling calm in the face of a difficult question or a presentation. There are any number of anchors we can use including: visual (eg a specific spot); voice (a specific phrase); or feelings (a specific touch). Anchors will be more effective if they are established in all of the visual, auditory and kinesthetic modes.

The other aspect of anchors is the effect on the learners: they will change state, reinforce learning, pay attention, or whatever else is appropriate when the anchor is applied. Comedians with gestures and catch phrases are particularly adept at this skill. As are actors and actresses who wish to create a certain state at a particular moment.

CREATING RAPPORT: EXERCISES

1. The trainer chooses to match and lead a learner in one or more of: body posture and movement, gestures, facial expression, language, eye accessing, cues, tone or tempo of pace.
   During the dialogue the trainer matches then leads the learner in one or more of the above. Evidence of success is if the learner follows the trainer's lead.
2. The trainer decides to match and then cross-over match a learner in one or more of the categories covered in 1.
   During dialogue the trainer matches then cross-over matches the learner. Evidence of success is then leading in the new cross-over way and the learner responding.
3. The trainer decides to match and lead the learner just using voice tone, pitch etc.
   During dialogue the trainer matches then leads the learner. Evidence of success is the learner following the lead.

CREATING RAPPORT: KEY POINTS

☐ Make a positive start.
☐ Fine-tune to physiology and posture.
☐ Use varied voice tonalities.
☐ Recognize learner language patterns.
☐ Use appropriate language patterns as a trainer.
☐ Observe and respond to breathing patterns.
☐ Use matching, cross-over matching and leading techniques.
☐ Recognize when you are in or out of rapport.
☐ Use anchors.

1.3 CREATING AND MAINTAINING HIGH EXPECTATIONS

Sometimes trainers can adversely impact on the quality of their training by setting too low a level of expectation with the trainees. This can be further compounded by the use of low impact, apologetic 'yes this is rather difficult' language. Some trainers become concerned about overhyping their training and as a consequence they actually undersell and devalue it.

Key steps to creating high expectations

1. Be clear about your own outcomes.
It is vital that the trainer is clear about what they themselves want to achieve from the training experience. No matter how many times the material has been taught, there should be a specific, tangible outcome for the trainer, either personally, professionally, or both.

2. Be clear regarding learner outcomes.
Obviously this is the key driver for the whole process. Learner outcomes might be personal, professional, organizational or social, and will almost certainly be mixed and varied in any particular group.

3. Use high energy materials at beginning.
This often takes the learners by surprise as they may be expecting a normal start to the training, eg the standard introduce self/each other beginning. Giving them a dynamic, high energy, all action start, tees them up for what is to come.

4. Use active language to engage trainees.
The purposeful use of language is a key part in NLP, and trainers will learn a great deal about themselves and their learners from awareness of its importance. Making learning fun and energetic, as well as useful, is one of the greatest achievements a trainer can make. It is very easy to create apathy in a room by using passive language and then blame the trainees for not being switched on, enthusiastic or motivated.

5. Be clear and honest about what can and cannot be achieved.
It is very easy in some circumstances to be unclear regarding what can or cannot be achieved. Either over- or under-hyping this will damage the effectiveness of the training. It is better to be honest and up-front with learners to help them achieve maximum benefit. Handled this way there will always be something for each learner to gain from the training.

6. Post short (session) and long (day or course) outcomes around the training room.
Sometimes learners (and trainers) think that the full benefit and impact from a training event will come together at the end. This can, obviously, be true, however, it is important to remember each stage of the journey as well. Everything worked on should move towards the end and flagging up the key steps along the way helps maintain interest, enthusiasm and allows learners to see where they are at, at a particular time.

7. Create an open environment.
In expecting a degree of openness from learners it is incumbent on the trainer to be the role-model and to set the tone and standard. This does not mean becoming over analytical or baring souls, but sharing experience, using self-disclosure and demonstrating that it is acceptable, and useful, to be open.

8. Relate everything you do back to the outcomes.
Let the learners see, hear and feel throughout that everything fits into the whole.

9. Show where you are in terms of overall outcomes.
Flag up every stage of the journey so that everyone can see what is happening.

10. Use your observations and skills to fine-tune learners.
Stay continually focused on the learners and where they are at. Use all sensory information available to be aware of them, both individually and collectively.

11. Match and lead whenever appropriate.
Do this to help move learners forward to achieve their outcomes (see 4.2 Pacing and leading a group, page 108).

12. Use humour wherever it is appropriate.
Humour is a very powerful ingredient in the trainer's portfolio. Humour should always be true to the trainer but, used properly, can not only create rapport with a group, but challenges and stimulates their thinking (see 4.6 Using humour, page 122).

13. Use a wide variety of training materials.
Keep the training varied, well paced, stimulating and offering a consistent (and purposeful) surprise (see 2.8 Using a variety of training techniques, page 51).

14. Create significant events along the way to help people retain information/insights.
Most journeys require some milestones and indications of progress. Training, even on short courses or programmes, is no exception. It helps individuals or groups to make sense of the journey and people remember the significant events, eg abseiling on an outdoor programme, a particular exercise, for the rest of their lives. Running a course or programme is like completing a jigsaw or building a wall, it takes place in stages. There will be lots of information and insights along the way that will help everyone understand faster and retain for longer. Any comment, question, example, piece of dialogue, even a break, may be of use.

15. Check regularly on levels of understanding.
It is very easy to achieve acquiescence and compliance in a group or to make assumptions about where they are in terms of their learning. Checking regularly ensures that all is going well.

16. Use pre-exposure to topics before going into them in more detail.
Any trainer with experience of NLP will know that a lot of teaching is done to the unconscious mind as well as the conscious mind, and that a lot of true learning is actually done at an unconscious level. Therefore, it is extremely useful to be able to pre-prepare the learner somewhere between 24 and 72 hours before the concrete experience itself takes place.

17. Research indicates that pre-exposure makes subsequent learning go more quickly.
If you pre-expose a group to a topic, piece of information or, even better, demonstrate a skill while ostensibly doing something else, or covering another topic, then, when the specific subject or skill is reached a couple of days later, learning will be faster, more powerful and more effective.

18. Use a variety of languages (eg visual, auditory and kinesthetic) to create a full picture in all senses.
A fundamental part of NLP is the role that the representation systems play. It requires skill and dexterity on the part of the trainer to (a) listen carefully to learners to ascertain their preferences, and (b) use the appropriate variety to help them achieve maximum learning, but it can be the difference that really makes the learning work.

19. Use embedded commands to tee up later activities.
Combining this technique with the pre-exposure to topics helps ensure a positive response to the subject at the later point as well as maximum learning (see 3.7 Using embedded commands, page 91).

20. Share your own outcomes with the group.

As we have said it is vital that the trainers are clear about their own outcomes from each particular event. It can also be helpful and useful to share them with a group, thereby creating a learning loop using the trainer as both a demonstration and a role-model.

21. Be open, up-front and honest with the group.

Unless this is seen to be done and believed in, the quality of any training and learning may well be adversely affected.

CREATING AND MAINTAINING HIGH EXPECTATIONS: EXERCISES

1. Practise paying close attention to own and learners' language, change use of language where appropriate.
2. Practise calibrating to individuals and groups of learners, seek feedback on your calibration skills. Based on your calibration, match and lead towards positive achievement of outcomes.
3. Use the opportunity to create reference experiences for learners.
4. Calibrate to learners' levels of understanding. Be prepared to do something different if necessary.
5. Practise giving pre-exposure to topics 24–72 hours before actually getting to a topic. Do this by 'walking the talk' on a particular topic, eg using meta model questions, matching and leading, using sleight of mouth in an open session.
6. Practise breaking out of your normal visual, auditory and kinesthetic (VAK) patterns for dealing with certain topics with certain groups (always calibrate to the group when doing this).
7. Practise using embedded suggestions, before and during, specific topics, or to open windows in the mind for later learning.
8. Be a role-model for all that you do (including handling the parts that don't work as well as they should).

CREATING AND MAINTAINING HIGH EXPECTATIONS: KEY POINTS

Creating high expectations:

- ☐ Be clear about your own outcomes.
- ☐ Be clear regarding trainee outcomes.
- ☐ Use high energy materials at beginning.
- ☐ Use active language to engage learners.
- ☐ Be clear and honest about what can and cannot be achieved.
- ☐ Post short (session) and long (day or course) outcomes around the training room.
- ☐ Create an open environment.

Maintaining high expectations:

- ☐ Relate everything you do back to the outcome.
- ☐ Show where you are in terms of overall outcomes.
- ☐ Use your observations and skills to fine-tune learners.
- ☐ Match and lead wherever appropriate.
- ☐ Use humour wherever it is appropriate.
- ☐ Use a wide variety of training materials.
- ☐ Create significant events along the way to help people retain information/insights.
- ☐ Check regularly on levels of understanding.
- ☐ Use pre-exposure to topics before going into them in more detail.
- ☐ Research indicates that pre-exposure makes subsequent thinking go more quickly.
- ☐ Use a variety of language, ie visual, auditory, kinesthetic, olfactory and gustatory to create a full picture in all senses.
- ☐ Use embedded suggestions to tee up later activities.
- ☐ Share your own outcomes with the group.
- ☐ Be open, up-front and honest with the group.

1.4 CREATING RITUALS AND ENGAGING EMOTIONS

There is a tendency, particularly in the UK, to be wary of showing and sharing emotions. The research which has been carried out over the last few years indicates very strongly that for trainees to retain information and/or go away and develop a new behaviour, some level of emotional engagement should have taken place. Dr James McGaugh, psychobiologist at UC Irvine, states that when emotions are engaged the brain is activated. This work has been followed up by O'Keefe and Nadel (1978) and Hooper and Terisi (1986), all of whom have endorsed the point. All of the work carried out since the development of NLP endorses how important this mind/body connection is.

For most people the key events they remember in life are the highs and the lows, eg school, holidays, relationships. Therefore, based upon the way the brain prefers to work it is vital to engage emotions. Rituals are the starting point for this. Rituals are a symbolic way of either creating a positive learning environment, illustrating that something important has just occurred, or drawing something to a conclusion.

Examples of rituals are:

- Using a certain track or type of music as people enter the room.
- Creating rules for the training process, eg if someone is late after a break they must deliver a two minute speech on a subject of the group's choice.
- Having a rule that if someone is bored they will put their hand up, you will stop, ask the group if the rest are bored, and if more than 25 per cent put their hands up, you agree to wind up that part of the topic within two minutes and move on.
- Relating back to the outcomes is an opportunity to create a ritual.
- Repetitive use of key phrases and words are rituals.
- Using humour effectively and relating it to the group is a ritual.
- Using role-play, greetings, debates, suspense, celebrations are also part of this process. Most NLP techniques have a form of ritual built into them.

Virtually all effective trainers use a lot of rituals, often without realizing it. Deliberately building them into the early part of the training, then repeating or building on them is a very powerful training technique and will allow trainees to show and share their emotions.

Most people recognize that although they 'know' something to be true change only happens when they 'feel' it to be true. This, once established, will lead to increased self-confidence and the desire to learn more. Anchoring these processes will enormously help this be achieved. Again, most effective training and NLP techniques create a strong kinesthetic, ie a feeling or sensation that goes with the changed state.

CREATING RITUALS AND ENGAGING EMOTIONS: EXERCISES

1. Practise using music at the beginning or during a training event.
2. Create fun rules for the training process.
3. Use key words and phrases in specific situations.
4. Use humour where appropriate.
5. Be prepared to use any of the relevant NLP techniques.
6. Use anchors.
7. Help learners become aware of their own rituals, particularly with regard to the learning process, or specially in certain situations, eg in a team session or when interviewing someone.

CREATING RITUALS AND ENGAGING EMOTIONS: KEY POINTS

☐ Create a series of highs for participants.
☐ Use music if appropriate.
☐ Create games and events.
☐ Create rules that involve people.
☐ Use key phrases and words at particular moments.
☐ Use humour appropriately.
☐ Use role-play, greeting, celebrations, etc.

CREATING RITUALS AND ENGAGING EMOTIONS: CASE STUDY

On a training course for 33 graduates which was geared toward self-managed learning, a piece of music called 'Search for the Hero Inside Yourself' was used as people entered the room for each session. Initially no one made the connection, then over the three days of the course people did.

The outcome of this was mass dancing and a group massage at any moment the group felt it needed energizing or refocusing. Since then a large number have acquired the music and use it as an anchor, or sing or hum it to themselves whenever they are working on some aspect of self-managed learning.

1.5 USING EXERCISE BURSTS TO CREATE ENERGY

Often training is delivered over quite long periods of time, which means that the energy levels of all those involved become stretched to the limit. Breaking training times down into one and a half to two hour bursts is a critical element in overcoming this fatigue.

Also left and right brain research (Klein and Armitage, 1979) indicates that there are alternating periods of efficiency for each side. In testing, the researchers found that verbal scores (left brain) improved from 165 to 215 and spatial (right brain) performance scores improved from 108 to 125 based on when they were taught. They also found that this alternated on 90 to 100 minute cycles, ie we switch from left to right brain and back again throughout the day.

This matches the discovery that people have ultradian rhythms known as BRAC (Break–Rest–Activity Cycle). This also fits in with our dream times and our patterns of REM (rapid eye movement).

Equally the time of day can have quite an impact on people's learning and memory capacity. The research of Brewer and Campbell (1991) indicates that from 9–11 in the morning the brain is 15 per cent more efficient for short-term memory; therefore, the morning is the best time for problem solving, report writing, maths and sciences. The time from noon to 2 o'clock is best for paperwork, music, singing, art and movement-based tasks, and from 2–5pm for theatre, history, literature, music and sports. In simple terms the morning is best for new information, the afternoon for integration.

Therefore, the trainer should do more passive activities based upon new learning in the morning and consolidate with a mix of more integrating type activities, eg exercises, simulations, role-play, presentations in the afternoon.

Freely (1984), Price (1980) and Virotsko (1983) discovered that no matter when you present a topic you are likely to 'miss' approximately one-third of your trainees. Therefore, anything that can be done to get or regain attention is a definite plus.

One of the many advantages of an awareness of NLP is the use of sensory acuity to help 'fine-tune' individuals or groups.

Exercise bursts include:

- getting up and moving around;
- stretch breaks every 30 minutes;
- jumping up and down;
- clapping;
- changing seats;
- dancing;
- mass massages;
- hopping;
- high fives;
- walking round the room five times;
- deep breathing;
- getting them to stand up for short bursts while you are presenting;
- cycling in their chairs.

Anyone, for example, in hobbies and sports, who has used energy bursts to create a different and better mental state knows how powerful these techniques can be. It has taken NLP, with its focus on how these factors come together and work, to bring them into the training arena.

USING EXERCISE BURSTS TO CREATE ENERGY: EXERCISES

1. Be prepared to try any of the exercise bursts listed in the section, eg stretch breaks, changing seats, massages.
2. Be a role-model for optimizing energy (if asked how you manage to maintain your energy, ask them how they manage to lose theirs).
3. Break up sessions into shorter cycles.
4. Practise balancing left and right brain activities (this includes sequencing them appropriately).
5. Help learners analyse and recognize the changed state exercise bursts create.

USING EXERCISE BURSTS TO CREATE ENERGY: KEY POINTS

☐ Break your training into 90-minute sections.
☐ Use materials that use both left and right brain.
☐ Use the BRAC (Break–Rest–Activity Cycle).
☐ Sequence your materials to achieve maximum effectiveness throughout the day.
☐ Use short, sharp exercise bursts.

1.6 ACKNOWLEDGING DIFFERENT LEARNER STYLES

Earlier in this chapter we mentioned the various ways that people prefer to learn, predominantly by using either Honey and Mumford's Learning Styles Questionnaire, or the Kolb Learning Styles Inventory.

The Honey/Mumford Learning Styles Questionnaire (LSQ) is the best known in the UK and is used already by many trainers and organizations, and has the benefit of using straightforward language and descriptions. By answering 80 questions, feedback is received on preferences ranging through Activist – Theorist – Reflector – Pragmatist.

In addition, with the use of the accompanying Manual of Learning Styles, there is a comprehensive back-up covering

- setting the scene for learning styles;
- administering, scoring and interpreting the LSQ;
- learning activities and learning styles;
- designing an off the job programme;

- helping to create personal development plans;
- designing learning to learn sessions;
- learning about yourself as a trainer;
- literature on learning styles.

The use of this information in the context of NLP is important. It shows that in learning, as in everything else, everybody does it their way (which may not be our way). It emphasizes the need for the trainer to use the full range of NLP techniques both to create and maintain personal flexibility, set outcomes, use sensory acuity and many others, as well as helping them stay very focused on the learners and develop strategies for them to achieve their outcomes.

At some point it would be very interesting and useful to apply the full range of NLP applications to these Learning Styles and get beneath the surface of them, modelling their effectiveness and what the key components are.

ACKNOWLEDGING DIFFERENT LEARNER STYLES: EXERCISES

1. Use the Honey-Mumford (or other) LSQ to help learners recognize different styles of learning.
2. Help learners recognize different strengths and weaknesses of each style.
3. Help learners develop greater flexibility of learning styles.
4. Use NLP calibration skills to help recognize different learner styles.
5. Use the relevant NLP techniques to help learners to develop flexibility, eg anchoring a resourceful state.
6. Use NLP techniques to develop learning strengths for the future.

ACKNOWLEDGING DIFFERENT LEARNER STYLES: KEY POINTS

- ☐ Consider use of a questionnaire, eg the LSQ.
- ☐ Be aware of the different ways that people learn.
- ☐ Be aware of own preferences relating to learning.
- ☐ Use any of the relevant NLP techniques to help the training be more effective.
- ☐ Balance materials with preferences of learners to both match and challenge.
- ☐ Embed learning using NLP.
- ☐ Help create patterns for future effective learning.
- ☐ Check with learners' VAK preferences.

CREATING AN EFFECTIVE PERSONAL STATE

CREATING AN EFFECTIVE PERSONAL STATE

'We are in truth more than half of what we are by imitation. The great point is to choose good models and to study them with care.'
Lord Chesterfield

In order for the training to have any chance of success it requires – like an effective interview, appraisal or meeting – preparation so that the trainer is in control of their own personal state. The consequences of not being so are lack of helpfulness and use to the learners, as well as loss of credibility. Fortunately there are a whole range of NLP techniques which help this process, and thereby also help the learners to achieve their own outcomes.

2.1 MAINTAINING A POSITIVE PERSONAL STATE

As has already been stated in the previous chapter, learners are influenced on a number of levels by trainers, and how they conduct themselves during training.

The trainer needs to maintain positive and congruent body language and remember that the research of Albert Mehrabian (1972) indicates that the emotional impact of a piece of communication can be broken down into:

    55%   body language
    38%   voice tone, pitch, pace, etc
     7%   actual words used.

Therefore, if there is any mixed signal and lack of congruency, the message received will be, at best, confused and, at worst, contradictory.

Visualizing is a technique used by many successful people including sports people, actors and actresses, politicians. This involves using the mind's eye to create a picture of the trainer performing an aspect of their role, eg giving a presentation, successfully. Also checking that the body language and words and voice are matched and adding to the success. Constant repetition of this picture will pre-programme the mind to ensure a successful presentation when the day itself arrives.

Going one step further and imagining the specific occasion, location, people will embed this even further (see 2.6 Using anchors, page 45, and 4.20 Using future pacing, page 166).

MAINTAINING A POSITIVE PERSONAL STATE: EXERCISES

1. Most people if they stood with one foot on two separate bathroom scales would find the scales registering different weights. This is because most people are not centred. In order to create a positive personal state it is useful to be centred and it also causes a positive impact on an audience. The simplest way to become centred is to stand with the feet six to nine inches apart and rock gently from side to side, initially as far as is comfortable, then slowing down until the movement is almost imperceptible, before finally stopping.

   Having done this concentrate on the area just below the navel and find what feels like the centre of the body. Finally, raise the body as if being pulled up by the hair until the centre is directly above the mid point between the feet. (This is also a useful quick exercise to use as an energy burst – see 1.5 Using exercise bursts to create energy, page 27.)

2. The second exercise is known as 'creating a trainer state'. Its purpose is to create an expanded sense of awareness, and steps to achieve this are:
   - focus on an object somewhere at the far end of the room, giving the object your total and absolute attention;
   - expand your sight and awareness to the two far corners, noticing everything in your vision;
   - draw your vision slowly down both side walls and then behind you, without moving your head, tuning in to everything you become aware of;
   - repeat three to four times as necessary.

   Doing this in an empty room prior to a training session is a very powerful way of creating a positive state and helps enormously when the room is filled with people. The depth of and subtlety of the information the trainer picks up can be astonishing. This exercise is also used by sales and sports people, and others who require a high sense of what is happening around them.

3. A third exercise was developed by Anthony Robbins in his book *Awakening the Giant Within*. Although not designed specifically for trainers it is very powerful. Anthony Robbins calls it the Ten Day Challenge.

   Rule 1: In the next *ten consecutive days* refuse to dwell on any unresourceful thoughts or feelings connected with training. Refuse to indulge in any disempowering questions or devitalizing vocabulary or metaphors.

Rule 2: When you catch yourself beginning to focus on the negative – and you certainly will – immediately redirect your focus towards a more positive emotional state. This will change your state, it does not ignore the problem but it keeps you in the right state while you identify what you need to do differently. Focus in the direction of establishing empowering mental and emotional patterns as you train. At the end of the day focus on what worked well to get into a great state before dropping off to sleep.

Rule 3: For the next ten consecutive days make certain that the whole focus on training is on *solution* and not problems. The minute you see a possible challenge, immediately focus on what the solution could be.

Rule 4: If you backslide – that is, if you catch yourself indulging in or dwelling on an unresourceful thought or feeling – do not beat yourself up. There is no problem with this as long as change is made immediately. However, if you continue to dwell on unresourceful thoughts or feelings, for any measurable length of time, it is necessary to wait until the following morning and start the ten days over again. The objective of the ten day challenge is *ten consecutive days* without holding or dwelling on a negative training thought. This starting over process must happen no matter how many days in a row the task has already been accomplished (copyright Anthony Robbins).

This latter exercise – once completed – is extremely powerful and enables the trainer to be very focused on success and achievement while impacting greatly on trainees.

In addition it is very useful to take energy from the group, to conserve one's own. This can be likened to surfing, where the key skill is hitting the wave at the right moment in order to achieve maximum effect.

Equally when things seem not to be going as well as hoped for, rather than throwing energy and emotion at a group, to get them moving use a little bit of 'trainer tai kwando', ie redirecting the flow of the training by taking the strength of the individual/group and refocusing it, by using questions and other techniques, this works very powerfully.

Other exercises for maintaining a positive personal state:

4. Mental rehearsal
    - Have an image of you as the trainer performing excellently (do this in a disassociated state). (See 2.14 Using association/disassociation, page 62.)
    - Step into, and become, that image, fully associated with the accompanying sounds, internal dialogue, feelings, emotions and sensations.
5. Affirmations
    - Use prepared relevant, positive sentences developed and practised prior to and during the training. (This can also tie in with 1 as well.)
6. Pre-practise key points of the training *before* the actual event in the environment the training will be delivered.

MAINTAINING A POSITIVE PERSONAL STATE: KEY POINTS

☐ Remember the 55 per cent body language, 38 per cent voice, 7 per cent words principle.
☐ Be congruent – avoid mixed signals.
☐ Use visualization.
☐ Use anchors.
☐ Use future pacing.
☐ Use centring.
☐ Use creating a trainer state.
☐ Use the ten day challenge.
☐ Use the group energy.
☐ Redirect the group energy flow.

MAINTAINING A POSITIVE PERSONAL STATE: CASE STUDY

On a recent training course the non-verbal signals from a part of the group were apathetic and casual. Over the period of the first morning this began to affect some of the rest of the group.

Over the break a conversation started regarding the purpose of the training and this small group stated a number of negative views so that the trainer could hear. Rather than get drawn into that specific conversation the trainer initially created rapport non-verbally, while at the same time matching language patterns.

Following this, by maintaining a positive personal state verbally and non-verbally herself, she got them to visualize the different situations that were coming up and how they would be able to respond more effectively to them.

Following the break she broke the group up into different syndicates, got them to agree their own, new, updated outcomes and the course moved on.

2.2 CREATING PERSONAL FLEXIBILITY

One of the paradoxes of being a trainer is that it is possible to preach flexibility while evidencing completely contradictory behaviours. At one level or another this causes confusion and uncertainty in the mind of the learner. On one hand they are being told to be or do one thing while getting tangible evidence of something different.

Most behavioural research indicates that human beings become *more* stereotyped in their behavioural responses when under extreme pressure. The difficulty of this is that most people believe the opposite to be the case, thus making it even less likely that they will respond with the appropriate flexibility. In the case of the trainer this can mean that the tougher the group or the harder the topic, the more they rely on a tried and trusted technique.

In essence there is nothing necessarily wrong with this approach. The problem is that in an ever, and faster, changing world even the trainer's best-loved ploys may become extremely visible to a group.

One of the basic principles of NLP is that if what you are doing isn't working, do something else, anything else.

This is a classic situation where the full range of NLP techniques can be employed. Not just in the audiences but in the trainer, it is very easy to get into a 'stuck' state, by lack of behavioural flexibility. Therefore, it is important to be willing to use an appropriate technique, and then another if necessary. One added bonus to this is that quite often one of the learners will recognize the trainer doing something different, that moves things forward, and ask about it during a break or comment on it in open forum. This doesn't mean that they necessarily know that something was 'wrong', just that things got better.

One key aspect of this is using personal flexibility, even when things are going well. Most trainers have had the experience of everything being perfect one moment then very quickly deteriorating and momentum being lost. It requires great nerve and skill to change things while they are still working, but it can be extremely useful. This is rather like the cricket captain who waits for his bowlers to have runs scored off them before changing them. The effective captain takes the bowler off the over *before* the runs are scored!

The inevitable question is how do they know when to do it? This is where the skills of NLP are so useful. As has been shown already, there are a multiplicity of ways and levels of recognizing what is actually taking place.

CREATING PERSONAL FLEXIBILITY: EXERCISES

1. Use exercises covered in Creating a positive personal state modified to Creating personal flexibility.
2. Creating personal flexibility exercise:
    - Sit in a quiet place, relax.
    - Decide on the aspect of flexibility required, eg fine-tuning a group, using humour etc.
    - Create a VAK scenario of you using the flexible skill required. Notice what you are doing that makes it work.
    - Do it again, adding to the skills employed. Again notice what works.
    - Be aware of everything happening to the you demonstrating the flexibility.
    - Anchor.
    - Future pace.
3. Do a version of 2. But breaking down the flexibility you are working on into its VAK components.
4. Do 2. But focusing on a flexible skill you have used well in the past and then expanding it into a new skill area.
5. Do 4. But stay with the skill just to find out what you were doing that worked.
6. Practise fixing anchors so that you are ready the next time you need to be flexible.

CREATING PERSONAL FLEXIBILITY: KEY POINTS

☐ Avoid becoming stuck.
☐ The tougher the group, the more flexibility you use.
☐ Be prepared to change something that isn't working.
☐ Be prepared to change – sometimes when something *is* working – to be even more effective.
☐ Use the group to help optimize personal flexibility.
☐ Be prepared to change *before* something goes wrong.
☐ Use the full range of NLP techniques.

2.3 BEING A LEARNING TRAINER

One constant theme of this book is the trainer as role-model, not to show off or pander to one's ego, but rather to live out the key messages in a demonstrable way. Nowhere is that more important than in being a learning trainer. Being prepared to illustrate and share previous learning experiences, showing what is happening currently and indicating future plans, are all key elements in this process. This will help create a powerful reference experience for the learners and will help them to be more open to developing their own learning skills. Being prepared to switch training style to suit circumstances also demonstrates the willingness to learn and make the extra effort to help others learn.

2.4 BEHAVIOUR MODELLING AND STRATEGIES

One of the best-known discoveries that NLP has produced is that regarding strategies and modelling.

The original work Richard Bandler and John Grinder did with Milton Ericson, Fritz Perls and Virginia Satir showed that people who had particular skills and exhibited certain behaviours used strategies to achieve them. Some of the strategies were conscious, a number were, or had become, unconscious.

Further work showed that everyone uses strategies in order to get things done, eg driving a car, tying a shoelace, making a presentation. Equally intriguingly it was found that people had strategies for the things that they 'could not do', ie someone who believed themselves to be poor with their hands, or bad with numbers, was operating to a certain set of strategies. Therefore, all human behaviour is based on strategies.

What are strategies?

Strategies are based on the representation systems and sub-modalities (see Chapter 4) and they are the sequence that the representations occur in and they result in the behaviour being carried out. For example in talking to a successful footballer: he had a very clear visual representation of himself scoring a goal and then a strong kinesthetic response to the auditory aspect of being applauded by the crowd and being touched, hugged and congratulated by his team mates.

BEING A LEARNING TRAINER: EXERCISES

Based upon this model, each aspect can be broken down and the exercises used for other skill areas in this book, eg:

- ☐ mental rehearsal;
- ☐ affirmations;
- ☐ skill practice;
- ☐ creating personal (learning) flexibility;
- ☐ anchors;
- ☐ future pace;
- ☐ language patterns;
- ☐ eye accessing cues;
- ☐ perceptual positions; and
- ☐ all the Chapter 4 'Being flexible to meet the needs' exercises.

BEING A LEARNING TRAINER: KEY POINTS

- ☐ Live out being a learning trainer.
- ☐ Share previous experience.
- ☐ Show current learnings.
- ☐ Indicate future learning plans and opportunities.
- ☐ Demonstrate learning flexibility.
- ☐ Switch training style to suit circumstances.

Someone else, who aspired to playing at the same standard, actually had the same sequence (ie visual, auditory, kinesthetic), but because their image was of missing the goal, the sub-modality components were different and resulted in perpetuating a disempowering belief about themselves, which made the problem even worse.

Subsequent work that was carried out with the same two players showed that, although the examples above are about the moment of scoring the goal (or not) and the response to it, there were equivalent differences in their strategies for getting themselves into a position where they could score the goal in the first place.

BEHAVIOUR MODELLING AND STRATEGIES: CASE STUDY

Two simple examples in a training context illustrate this point. Someone on a training course has a strategy for learning that starts with:

1. imagining what the learning will be like when it has been used. In NLP terms this would be Visual Internal Constructed, written as V^I_C
2. seeing the steps that need to be taken to achieve it – Visual External V^E
3. telling themselves it's now time to get started – Auditory Internal Dialogue A^{ID}.
4. remembering the good feeling when it is completed – Kinesthetic Internal Remembered K^I_R

Therefore the strategy sequence for this behaviour would be written as:

$$V^I_C \longrightarrow V^E \longrightarrow A^{ID} \longrightarrow K^I_R$$

Someone else might, facing the same situation, go through it in quite a different way because they are not feeling positive about the learning process, eg:

1. sees possible negative consequences – Visual Internal Constructed V^I_C
2. asks themselves what will happen if I don't do this? – Auditory Internal Dialogue A^{ID}
3. looks at what *has* to be done – Visual External V^E
4. feels unhappy about it all – Kinesthetic Internal K^I

The strategy sequence for this behaviour is:

$$V^I_C \longrightarrow A^{ID} \longrightarrow V^E \longrightarrow K^I$$

From the trainer's point of view the approach required to match, pace and lead these two strategies is quite different. Knowledge of the codings (or notation as they are called in NLP) is helpful but not essential. What is useful is the insight into how people are doing what they do. This relates very clearly with the section on Meta Programs. (See 4.21 Using Meta Programs, page 167.)

The three components of a strategy are:

1. The beliefs that support the behaviour.
2. The physiology of the behaviour.
3. The strategies that support the behaviour.

The relationship could be described as:

Meta Programs   –   why learners do things
Strategies   –   how they do things

For those trainers who wish to know how to find out someone's strategy (strategy elicitation in NLP), the steps are:

1. Identify the specific behaviour.
2. Get the person to actually do the behaviour, or, as this is often not possible, get them to go back to a time when they were doing the behaviour and go into the state of doing it, in an associated way.
3. Identify the very first thing they are aware of as they are reliving the behaviour.
4. Find out what representation system they are using.
5. Establish whether the representation system is internal or external, remembered or constructed.
6. Identify the second thing they are aware of as they are reliving the behaviour.
7. Find out what representation system they are using.
8. Establish whether the representation system is internal or external, remembered or constructed.
9. Repeat until total strategy is elicited.

Points to remember in eliciting strategies

- Pay attention to predicates.
- Pay attention to eye accessing cues.
- Based on the first two points, choose appropriate questions, eg 'What were you feeling as you looked down there?'
- Help them to fill in any gaps by asking if there was anything else happening at the time.
- Pay close attention to sub-modality differences, eg seeing an image that is close, colourful and bright will produce a different response than one which is very grey, small and a long way off.

In their book *Training with NLP*, John Seymour and Joseph O'Connor outline an exercise they use to help trainers develop the skill of creating states. This can then usefully be followed by working through the strategies that the trainers utilized.

1. Each person (four in a group) thinks of three states they would like to be able to elicit in the groups they train. Each state is written down on a separate piece of paper and folded so the writing is not visible.
2. Each person puts their three target states into the middle to form a pool of 12 target states.
3. The first person takes the role of trainer for the group. They take a random piece of paper from the middle and attempt to elicit the state from the other three people in the group, who do not know what the state is. Trainers stop when they think they have succeeded, or after about one minute, no more, and ask what sequence of states each person has experienced.
4. Each person briefly indicates the states they went through and the state they finished in. Their task is *not* to guess the target state, but simply to respond to what the trainer does.
5. If the trainer is successful in eliciting the target state then it is another person's turn. If not, then the trainer tells the group what the target state was. The group then demonstrates to the trainer how they would look and sound if they were indeed in that state. The trainer takes note of this and can try again for up to a minute.
6. Each person takes a turn at the trainer role.

This exercise is a very good one in its own right. It can also be used to elicit the specific strategies that the trainer used to elicit the various states.

Like many parts of NLP this exercise can be used on a number of levels. For example, to develop personal flexibility, use anchors, practise language patterns, develop sensory acuity, create rapport, etc. It also illustrates the relevance of the whole field of modelling and strategies. Everything the trainer does is driven by a strategy, this strategy can be elicited and then either passed on to others or, for the purposes of this book, used to create an effective personal state. In other words, the trainer can *self-model* and then, based on the results, work to develop their own personal state.

This whole field is a vital part of NLP and can be applied to all aspects of life. For the purposes of this book this is as far as it needs to be taken.

BEHAVIOUR MODELLING AND STRATEGIES: EXERCISES

1. Use the two exercises covered in this section.
   - eliciting a strategy;
   - creating a trainer state.
2. Use the eliciting strategy exercise on self and others on:
   - normal day to day activities, eg tying a tie, starting a car etc;
   - NLP-based activities, eg creating rapport, anchors, language patterns.

This will be a generative process and will help develop the skills of strategies while also giving greater insight into NLP skills and techniques.

BEHAVIOUR MODELLING AND STRATEGIES: KEY POINTS

- ☐ Everybody has strategies for everything they do.
- ☐ People also have strategies for things they 'cannot do'.
- ☐ Strategies are the sequence in which the representation systems and sub-modalities take place.
- ☐ Strategies have three components:
  - beliefs;
  - physiology;
  - strategies that support the behaviour.
- ☐ There is a specific process to go through to elicit strategy.
- ☐ Behaviour modelling is taking an effective strategy and helping someone else acquire it.
- ☐ Behaviour modelling can be used on self for any purpose, here specifically to create an effective personal state.

2.5 SETTING OWN PERSONAL OUTCOMES

In keeping with the themes of this book, the setting of own personal outcomes for the trainer is a key factor. How can trainers know if they have succeeded, and measure that success, unless they have their own outcomes?

These outcomes can be personal, based on the content, or learner responses, or any other yardstick. The important point is that they are purposeful, have integrity and achieve the NLP guidelines for outcomes.

The personal outcomes process is:

1. Positive: Goal expressed in positive terms (not I don't want to lose control of a group but I want to achieve 98 per cent success on the feedback forms).

2. Own part: Can I 'actually' control the achievement of the outcome (rather than having to rely on someone else)?

3. Specific: Is the outcome tangible and measurable? Ask open questions of yourself.

4. Evidence: How will I know I have achieved the outcome? Use sensory specific, VAKOG language, eg I will hear a round of applause, see smiling nodding faces, feel warm in my chest.

5. Ecology: Do I really want the outcome? Does it fit in with other goals, with family, work, friends? Does it have honesty and integrity? Am I really committed?

6. Action: Start to do it now.

SETTING OWN PERSONAL OUTCOMES: EXERCISES

Use outcome process on key aspects of life and work and then extend it into other areas as needed.

SETTING OWN PERSONAL OUTCOMES: KEY POINTS

☐ Have appropriate personal outcomes established.
☐ Use NLP process for creating outcomes.
☐ Review and update outcomes as appropriate.

2.6 USING ANCHORS

Anchors can be used all through the training process and for a number of purposes. The best description of an anchor is *a process by which we make associations between experiences* – eg hearing a pleasant piece of music and being reminded of a place or a person, or seeing photographs which evoke specific memories or feelings. Other examples would be your wedding day or the funeral of a close friend. A particular face, comment or feeling will bring the memories flooding back.

The brain makes these associations of its own accord. The trainer has the opportunity to create these associations, build on them and use them to assist the learner in learning and making behavioural changes. These anchors can impact dramatically on the effectiveness of anyone involved in helping people to learn.

One way of using anchors is to be aware of the point you are making – ie is it a deep point, are you just conveying information, are you summarizing, etc? and anchor these both in specific locations in the room and by voice tonality, gesture, body posture, etc. This anchoring means that at quite a deep level you have created an association and a response. Therefore, in the future you can simply relive your part of the association and achieve your outcome.

The process of anchoring is used by many people who rely on personal performance including sports people, musicians, business people, creative people, as it allows for people to create and maintain their own personal state, as well as bring it all together for a peak moment. Sports people often refer to the 'white moment' when everything just comes together and flows and they are almost beyond themselves, everything is in place and working. This is an example which everyone has had at some time in some aspect of their life. The key is being able to recreate it, at will.

The key steps in resource anchoring are:

1. Identify a resource state you want as a trainer, eg confidence, poise, humour.
2. Find a specific occasion in your life when you felt confident (or whatever else you want).
3. Go back to that moment, relive the state you were in and remember what you could see there, what you could hear and what your feelings were. Then come back to the here and now, decide what anchors you want that will recreate the resourceful feeling. These should be visual, auditory and feelings, eg a specific visual image, a specific word and a specific gesture or touch, eg pulling an ear lobe, touching the right knee. These are your anchors.
    Note: For anchors to be really effective they work best if they are visual, auditory and kinesthetic, plus olfactory and gustatory if appropriate.
4. In your mind's eye put yourself fully back into the resource state you want. See what you could see, hear what you could hear and be fully in touch with your body and feelings. If there is a sequence of events relive them in that sequence, if there is a certain body position or aspect of physiology re-acquire that.

5. Just as the resourceful feeling is totally coming together and peaking, connect up (fire) all your anchors, ie see your specific image, hear/ say your specific word and make your specific gesture or touch (ensure that you did these three at the peak moment and you will have created a resource anchor for that personal resource state).
6. Repeat the above step five or six times to really build the connection.
7. Test the anchors. See the picture, hear the sound and make the gesture. Be very aware of how this brings back the resourceful state. If it does not feel quite right go back and repeat steps 4–5 as many times as necessary. Then test the anchors again.
8. Mentally rehearse your anchors prior to training.
9. Use the anchor during the actual training.

There are a number of key points to bear in mind regarding anchoring:

- The process of building and using resource anchors is a generative process, ie they become easier and more effective the more you use them.
- Just putting an anchor in place and then firing it six months later may work but success is much greater with practice.
- Firing anchors immediately prior to a specific training situation is very powerful.
- You can have anchors for as many situations as is required. In fact the more situations you have a specific anchor for the better.

The other vital part of anchoring is utilizing them for learners. Using space, location, voice tonality, specific words and phrases, gestures and mannerisms will all create anchors for your individuals and groups. They will come to recognize (probably at an unconscious level) that you are about to say something of vital importance when you drop your voice tone towards the end of the preceding sentence or when you move in a particular way or use a certain gesture. This is one example where creating an effective personal state will help the trainer, but also generate and demonstrate behavioural flexibility to a group and, therefore, help them do it for themselves.

Another important aspect is getting groups/individuals to create their own anchors to embed the learning, re-access or apply it. This combination ensures that training is fun as well as putting ownership for learning firmly where it belongs – with the learner.

USING ANCHORS: EXERCISES

Use anchoring process in a generative way in a wide variety of contexts and situations inside and outside the training area.

USING ANCHORS: KEY POINTS

☐ Use anchors to create positive associations.
☐ Use location to create anchors.
☐ Use voice tone to create anchors.
☐ Establish resourceful anchors for yourself.
☐ Keep building on the anchors.
☐ Use anchors before, as well as during, training.
☐ Use as many anchors as you need.
☐ Use space, words, phrases, gestures and mannerisms to create learning anchors for trainees.
☐ Get trainees to establish their own anchors for during the training and afterwards.

USING ANCHORS: CASE STUDY

A colleague was preparing for a very important course with a new client. The course was a pilot, and if successful, would lead to a great deal more work in the future.

In preparing for the course he decided, based upon the outcomes agreed, on the key issues and points that would make the day succeed. Arriving early, he established spatial anchors for himself when dealing with the key issues, as well as the voice tone and non-verbal gestures and mannerisms he would employ.

In addition he created a series of resource anchors for himself to use before and at regular intervals throughout the session.

The day went off as well as he hoped and the feedback from the group, and the HR Manager who had sat in on the course, was positive.

2.7 USING PERCEPTUAL POSITIONS

Perceptual positions are a very powerful aid to the trainer and one which allows for not getting caught up in the here and now, particularly when the here and now is negative. It also allows for an unusual form of coaching (of the trainer/by the trainer) while actually doing the training.

There are a number of perceptual positions. For the purposes of the trainer, the first three are enough.

First position

Our own personal point of view, our own reality, what we think as an individual from our own experience.

Second position

The other person in the interactions point of view. How it looks, sounds and feels from another person's point of view. Some people do not like this as they assume that if they understand what is happening to someone else they will have to agree with it. This is not the case, understanding is sufficient in its own right. Remember the old Indian motto: 'If you want to know a man properly walk a mile in his shoes'.

The other interesting point is that very strong rapport can often create a very good, clear second position.

Third position (sometimes known as Meta position)

This is the observer position. This is the ability to watch yourself (and other people involved) from the outside. Most people have had the experience of being outside themselves looking in. Third position is doing it at will, on purpose.

The advantages of being able to use all three perceptual positions are enormous. First position allows for staying totally in tune with yourself (see 2.1 Maintaining a positive personal state, page 33). Second position allows for really fine-tuning individuals/groups. This then allows for an intervention, eg change of approach, asking a question, speeding up, going deeper and, of course, it can be checked out openly with people, eg 'My feeling about what is happening, or, your requirement right now is...'.

Third position allows trainers to 'watch themselves, watching them'. This benevolent dispassion allows for advice to be given and accepted by you in first position from yourself in third position. This may sound a little bizarre but one exercise to develop the skill is:

- Imagine yourself in a recent training situation.
- Imagine the occasion as if on a stage or a TV screen with you in the audience watching the you on the stage or TV.
- Decide on a piece of advice that would help you on the stage or screen.
- Offer the advice in the third person, step back and allow yourself to receive the advice.

This technique is used extensively by comedians, actors, sports people to self-coach themselves on an ongoing basis. This is the key to self-awareness and personal development.

Another powerful use is to keep a deliberate overview on the whole training and dipping into a third position to ensure that the right things are happening or realign an approach if need be.

USING PERCEPTUAL POSITIONS: EXERCISES

Do the exercise covered, in a wide variety of contexts and situations, both inside and outside the training arena.

USING PERCEPTUAL POSITIONS: KEY POINTS

- ☐ Use first position to control own state.
- ☐ Use second position to understand others' feelings and views.
- ☐ Use third position to 'self-coach' regularly.
- ☐ Use third position to monitor trainer and training effectiveness.
- ☐ Use perceptual positions to self-develop.

USING PERCEPTUAL POSITIONS: CASE STUDY

In my early years of working with NLP, I was working with a new client on designing a training programme for his business. Although I had been recommended to him and we got along well, the process seemed stilted and difficult.

In preparing for the meeting that would decide the success or failure of the whole project, I decided to try a version of the exercise covered in this section.

In this situation I realized that I was rushing him, not giving him enough detail and not allowing him to contribute as much as he wanted to. The advice, therefore, was to give him a lot more information to consider, create time for him to digest it, and draw out his ideas. This was carried out, an enjoyable and successful meeting held, followed by successful completion of the training programme.

Note

In relaying this story to a number of non NLP-ers they said there was nothing special about that, it was just common sense, and anyone who was good at their job would have done it.

This is, of course, absolutely true, but proves that one key part of NLP is in putting a framework explanation and technique to *what works*.

2.8 USING A VARIETY OF TRAINING TECHNIQUES

It is essential that a successful trainer has the ability and confidence to use as wide a variety of training techniques as possible. It can be very easy to fall into the trap of repeating material, quotes and strategies that have produced good results previously and relying on them to work their magic once again.

As the training market becomes more and more sophisticated, so do a lot of the learners, and if the person doing the training is not 'walking the talk' ie visibly demonstrating their own flexibility, ability to respond to a variety of situations, being a willing learner themselves, taking risks and being open, then the effect and credibility of the training will also suffer.

This will involve using, at appropriate times, all of the types of resources covered in this book. Knowing you have a wide repertoire of materials also helps ensure that you create and maintain an effective personal state.

USING A VARIETY OF TRAINING TECHNIQUES: EXERCISES

Practise using the techniques covered in this book.

USING A VARIETY OF TRAINING TECHNIQUES: KEY POINTS

☐ Constantly research new materials.
☐ Be willing to try them out, even at the expense of old favourites.
☐ Share training experiences and materials with other trainers.
☐ If possible write, change materials, to match specific requirements.

2.9 USING CONTEXT AS WELL AS CONTENT CLUES

It can be very easy for trainers to deal only with knowledge and skills at a content level. The outcome of this is that trainees only retain the knowledge and skills at a surface level and real skill development and/ or behavioural change does not take place.

For knowledge and skills to become embedded it is vital for trainees to understand the context that surrounds the issue. This is because trainees will bring their own values and beliefs to any given situation, including how they prefer to be taught, and context deals with issues at a beliefs and values level. This is a fundamental aspect of using NLP to help achieve greater effectiveness in training.

Some training is based on dealing with content first and then following up with context. This means quite often that the focus is on the trainer 'getting it right', ie getting all the facts in, and in the correct sequence. The attention actually works better if it focuses on the trainee. This involves the ability to second position (see 2.7 Using perceptual positions, page 48) effectively while retaining a strong first position by asking yourself the following questions:

- Is it *what* I'm saying?
- Is it *how* I'm saying it?
- Is it the *circumstances* around us?

Dependent on the response to these questions the trainers should *change what they are doing.*

Therefore, allowing the trainees to have the experience first allows them to question and analyse the experience from a deeper level of knowledge and use rather than 'following the rules'. This is a difficult and unnatural step for many trainers when they feel as though they are losing control in some way. But it also means that the subsequent review will bring out a wider and deeper level of questions than the normal, conventional process.

Achieving this can also be difficult because it means that trainees are also, initially at least, facing the unknown and it may take some getting used to. Recent research evidence (Caine and Caine, 1991) shows that the brain is operating on many levels at the same time and prefers to work this way. Also the work of Botella and Eriksen (1992) shows the way the brain uses parallel processing in a variety of tasks. Francis Crick, the Nobel Prize-winning scientist, states that very little learning takes place in a neat, orderly manner, and says that the functions of the brain 'are usually massively parallel' (Crick, 1994). Eric Jensen in his book *The Learning Brain* states that: 'what learners are normally left with are basic chunks of information: the unit of knowledge or experience and the pattern. Facts may provide the answer on a text, but the pattern equals real meaning for life.'

In addition, using context as well as content clues gives the bigger picture and engages the curious, intuitive right brain as well as the logical, analytical left brain. This means that the relevance and impact of the content, used in its proper place, will achieve greater results for the trainee.

USING CONTEXT AS WELL AS CONTENT CLUES: EXERCISE

Give learners an experience before giving them the theory.

USING CONTEXT AS WELL AS CONTENT CLUES: KEY POINTS

☐ Give the big picture context clues before content.
☐ Be aware of trainees' values and beliefs.
☐ Give trainees the context, then the experience, then the content.
☐ Use second position skills to fine-tune individuals/groups.
☐ Be self-aware – ask yourself:
  – Is it *what* I'm saying?
  – Is it *how* I'm saying it?
  – Is it the circumstances around us – if so, change what you are doing.
☐ Be prepared for deeper level review and questions.
☐ Engage the brain on multi-levels.
☐ Create big picture patterns for trainees' multi-facets.
☐ Engage right brain as well as left brain.

USING CONTEXT AS WELL AS CONTENT CLUES: CASE STUDY

A few years ago a training was being carried out for a group of scientists who were just taking over their own teams for the first time.

On the course they were hungry for models and rules that they could apply on their return to work. The training was carried out, much to their alarm, by putting them into situations where they had the experience, reviewed the content, established the context they were working in, and then, based upon sound principles, developed their own strategies for back at work.

Although this approach had caused some initial concern, by the end of the process they commented on how much more, and better, sense the topic now made.

2.10 USING THE BIG PICTURE/LITTLE PICTURE TECHNIQUE

It is very important to ensure that trainees are able to make sense on a number of levels of the points the trainer is putting across. This involves explaining the big picture – eg major trends in business today, the strategy plan for the organization – and then putting in the specific steps/information which gives all of the detail.

The reason for using this technique is that people sort information into different sizes and shapes or 'chunks', primarily into specifics or generalities. A lot of the mismatch between a trainer and groups or individuals is because one party is operating on one level of detail and the other on another level.

People who 'chunk' down into specifics tend to:

- break things down into small parts;
- concentrate on details;
- miss the overall picture;
- like details in sequence;
- like concrete examples.

In discussions or questions they tend to:

- give you all the details and go very deep into explanation;
- talk about the steps and sequences;
- go back to the beginning if distracted or interrupted;
- use words like – exactly, precisely, specifically, plan, schedule, order, organized, definite.

People who 'chunk up' into generalities tend to:

- talk in concepts and ideas;
- concentrate on the overall direction of a project or task;
- want the big picture first;
- summarize tasks and events;
- not like step-by-step procedures.

In discussions or questions they tend to:

- present the concept or idea first;
- get easily bored with details;
- leap ahead of detailed subject matter;
- read 'in between the lines' and come to different conclusions;
- use words like – generally, basically, overall, framework, idea, concept, flexible.

Bearing in mind that most people, even though they have a preferred tendency, will use some of each, it is vital that the effective trainer covers both the big picture and fills in the appropriate detail. Only dealing with one or the other will mean that trainees will get demotivated, demoralized, blame the trainer (or themselves) and the whole process will be weakened.

Visual aids including slides, posters, video will often provide the big picture which is then supported by exercises, discussion, handouts to provide more of the detail. Different audiences will also have different preferences, eg accountants are likely to be small picture focused, and designers more likely to be big picture, although, like all generalizations, this should not be taken too literally. Fine-tune to the individual/group.

Even though audiences may, due to job or background, have a clear preference it is still important that the trainer uses the big picture and small picture approach to help trainees learn more effectively.

USING BIG PICTURE/LITTLE PICTURE TECHNIQUE: EXERCISES

1. Structure training to start with big picture, then go into detail, then revisit big picture at end.
2. Practise and measure quality of response and learning.

USING BIG PICTURE/LITTLE PICTURE TECHNIQUE: KEY POINTS

☐ Recognize whether group/individuals are big/little picture.
☐ Gear your approach accordingly.
☐ Use materials to create big picture, eg visual aids.
☐ Use input, discussion, handouts to fill details.
☐ Have a balance between big and little picture.
☐ Recognize that some groups are more likely to be big or little picture.
☐ Ask questions at both a big and little picture level to check learning and understanding and to create rapport.

2.11 UNDERSTANDING BRAIN HEMISPHERE FUNCTIONS

One of the major breakthroughs in recent years which really assists the trainer is the work done on brain hemispheres. Dr Roger Sperry, the Nobel Prize winner, was the first to explain the different ways the parts of the brain prefer to operate (Sperry, 1968). The difficulty is that some of this work has been clouded by factions stating that either left or right brain is the better way to be. This ignores the point that the brain prefers to use *both* sides but in different ways and circumstances.

It is now widely accepted that the left side of the brain is the more logical, calculating, sequential side, while the right prefers initiative and creativity. But on what does the intuitive right brain base its intuition? Often on facts analysed by the logical left side. In training, therefore, it is vital to provide enough 'big picture' materials to appeal to both sides before structuring the rest of the training in more specific ways. NLP techniques and processes help to achieve this.

The brain works on a 'whole' basis supported by different emphases for differing processes and topics. It also deals with a huge amount of situations and information at the same time. In addition, it seems to prefer operating in this way rather than in a step-by-step way.

There is a wealth of evidence that exercise and physical bursts of energy stimulate brain responses. This can be where the energy bursts and other techniques covered elsewhere (see 1.5 Using exercise bursts to create energy, page 27) can be so effective. This is also where the full range of training materials and techniques become crucial, because they engage both sides of the brain and at a multiplicity of levels. A balance between activities ensures that the trainer does not make the mistake of only utilizing the straight ahead left side, or the more whimsical and intuitive right side.

Another piece of interesting research has been undertaken that shows that language can have a remarkable impact on the brain and the various moods of the learner (Kotulak, 1993). An example of this was quoted with a learner being downhearted. The appropriate words used by the trainer caused a response in the learner's brain which resulted in a positive change in mood and reaction. This is where the feedback sandwich can be so powerful. It is essential that the trainer is doing this with integrity, is pacing and leading the learner and has a positive objective to work towards.

This aspect relates to the internal dialogue of the trainer and the learner. Creating and using more self-empowering internal dialogue will help to move things forward for all those who are involved.

Other research indicates that learners and trainers become programmed into certain responses. This is normally based on a protection factor to avoid certain circumstances and becomes embedded and automatic to situations. The trainer is queried over something they either believe totally in or are not absolutely sure about. They give a conditional response, based upon previous experience, and the response becomes stored and even more embedded for the next time, and so it goes on. Flexibility is lost, and so quite often is the learner.

Equally this can also apply to the learner, particularly in areas of fear or concern. They will not necessarily analyse their response in a balanced way, but may well rationalize the behaviour and find reasons to justify it.

Some research has been carried out that indicates that feelings and moods can affect attitude, and response, to effective training. If the learner is feeling downhearted or depressed about themselves or their situation it may, initially, make them harder to deal with.

Having said that, one of the great benefits of NLP techniques is that almost all of them are able to change the trainer's and learner's state. This combined with the powerful effect of good training materials really adds to the trainer's repertoire.

It is, therefore, vital for the effective trainer to know about, recognize and respond to the various ways that the impact of the brain operations may have on the learner. To that end some basic facts can be useful:

- The brain contains 10–15 million nerve cells, all of which are different.
- Each of these has up to ten thousand ways of linking or moving information.
- The brain uses up to one-fifth of the oxygen intake.
- The corpus callosum, which joins the various parts of the brain together, has approximately 300 million conductors for moving information around the brain.
- Research suggests that from the age of 25 we lose 100,000 brain cells a day; this still means people have more than enough to use effectively, even into advanced old age.

Most people have a predominance, using one side of the brain more than the other. It is also important to remember that the brain/body connection works 'the wrong way round' ie the right side of the brain controls the left side of the body.

Some of the differences between the two sides of the brain are:

Right brain
Does everything at once, holistic, looks for/makes connections, instinctive, intuitive, likes images, not interested in time.

Left brain
Likes things in sequence, separates into detail, breaks things down, looks for specific conclusion, deduces by reason, likes grammar/words, time focused.

Again the point should be made clear that although in most people the right and left brains work in this way, in a small number they are the other way round. Also that effective training will, dependent on the audience and the subject, be best learnt by using both sides of the brain as appropriate.

This also has implications for the physical body. Most people use one eye more than the other. They also distribute their weight and body posture differently. A simple way to assess this is to stand on two pairs of bathroom scales simultaneously and see if they weigh the same. In many cases the difference is up to a stone. This is not just due to the distribution of the body organs, most people favour one side or the other for certain functions. (See 2.1 Maintaining a positive personal state, page 33.)

Most of these postures and the movements that accompany them have become habitual in the individual, normally without them being aware of it. NLP, and other disciplines, eg the Alexander Technique, Feldenkrist, Rolfe, have some very effective ways of dehabitualizing people and creating more physical flexibility.

These issues become important in the learning situation because many learners have also developed habitual learning patterns, influenced by their brain function preferences. Like most patterns the person least aware of them is likely to be the individual, so trainers should use their own flexibility to best effect while realizing it may be new territory for the learner.

Due to the western world focus on language, which is normally a left brain function, the importance of the right brain was ignored for many years. This was particularly due to the fact that if someone has an illness such as a stroke, it is the impact on their use of language which is most obvious to people.

In addition most normal education has been based on, and made best use of, the functions of the left side of the brain. The types of information and the way they are presented has reinforced the left brain dominance and made people wary of using and trusting the more 'intuitive' right brain. Many organizations in the UK and around the world are now, slowly, becoming aware of this and trying to 'retrain' managers back into right brain skills. As ever with these issues children, particularly in their very early years, appear to be able to use both sides of the brain appropriately and only move towards a reliance on one side as they grow up and are educated. This means that they learn to trust logic and analysis over intuition, ie head over heart.

One of the interesting dynamics of these factors is that new discoveries can be made by both sides of the brain, so that although it would sound thematically likely that the right brain would make the initial discovery which would then be validated by the left brain, it's just as likely that discoveries will be made by logical, deductive, analysis, arriving at the correct conclusion. This may be partially caused by the right brained person having moved on to the next situation or idea.

In traditional learning, left brained people have had a preference for subjects such as sciences, mathematics and engineering; while right brained people have preferred design, music and art. Other subjects are likely to be more middle of the road. History, for example, can appeal because it is based on facts and is sequential, or because it excites the imagination.

Equally, regarding jobs, certain predictions will have a truth (although not the whole truth). So a list of jobs based upon brain dominance would be:

Right brain
Designer, photographer, architect, actor.

Left brain
Computer programmer, accountant, engineer, solicitor.

Designing and delivering training programmes for people from all these functions which will work for them is one of the great arts of the good trainer. It can also be a factor for HR staff designing job advertisements to appeal to specific candidates, and then to the questions asked during the actual interview process.

There are a number of techniques available which appeal to both sides of the brain. The mindmapping work developed by Tony Buzan is one such technique.

The generally accepted guidelines for mindmapping are:

- Start in the centre of the page with the topic.
- Using whatever comes into the head, branch out from the centre, put a name to the branch line.
- Printed words should be on lines and each line connected to other lines.
- Put everything down without worrying about appearance or presentation.
- After completion check links and connect up.
- Use different colours to distinguish between primary branches.
- Use as many shapes, symbols, colours, etc as is useful.

The benefits of mindmapping are:

- greater definition of the main idea;
- more important ideas are clearer as they will be nearer to the centre;
- new information is easy to add;
- the corrections are more visible.

This process uses the freethinking, brainstorming right brain and the logical, developmental, planned left brain to optimize the performance of each.

Other whole-brain techniques in this book include visualizing, future pacing and anchoring.

It is useful for the trainer to be aware of, and respond to, their own left and right brain preferences. If trainers are left brained and prefer very logical, structured, sequential training they need to be clear regarding the implications of this for the learning group. Equally if they intuitively prefer the more holistic, intriguing type of training this also will have to be married to the learning needs of the audience.

UNDERSTANDING BRAIN HEMISPHERE FUNCTIONS: EXERCISES

1. Practise analysing, preparing and delivering training based on both hemisphere functions.
2. Practise looking for evidence of preferences for left or right brain uses in particular individuals, groups, job types, organizations.
3. Use materials and language based on both hemisphere functions and response and effectiveness.
4. Practise these skills outside the training arena.

UNDERSTANDING BRAIN HEMISPHERE FUNCTIONS: KEY POINTS

☐ Left brain is more logical and calculating.
☐ Right brain is more creative and intuitive.
☐ Both sides are vitally important for effective learning.
☐ The brain prefers to multi-process.
☐ Energy bursts help the brain perform more effectively.
☐ A wide variety of materials and techniques helps cover all the ways the brain likes to work.
☐ Language can reflect and impact on the brain's process.
☐ Creating more self-empowering internal dialogue helps the learning process.
☐ The brain can be programmed into certain responses.
☐ Most learners have a preference for being left or right brained.
☐ A lot of traditional learning was left brain based.
☐ Mindmapping is so effective because it uses both left and right brain functions.
☐ Most NLP techniques use both left and right brain functions.
☐ Trainers should be aware of their own left and right brain preferences.

2.12 USING CALIBRATION

Calibration is a baseline NLP skill. A definition of calibration is: *reading, fine-tuning and being sensitive to a person or group's non-verbal behaviour.* In order to achieve effective calibration it is necessary to pay high-quality attention to learners' physiology. It also requires being in 'uptime' ie focused outwards, and picking up on and recognizing relevant signals. Like all of the NLP skills many trainers will already do this naturally and instinctively.

USING CALIBRATION: EXERCISES

1. Take a particular facet, eg breathing, and calibrate to an individual, group or whole course.
2. Take another facet and do the same, eg:
   - physiology;
   - gestures;
   - postures;
   - eye accessing cues;
   - voice tone, pitch, pace, etc.
3. Start to combine the above until doing all of them becomes habitual.
4. Start to notice the moment of change (ie when do learners shift their posture, use certain mannerisms?).

USING CALIBRATION: KEY POINTS

☐ A baseline NLP skill.
☐ Based on non-verbal behaviour.
☐ Requires paying high quality attention.
☐ Need to be in uptime, ie focused outwards.

USING CALIBRATION: CASE STUDY

On an appraisal skills training course one person was very quiet and detached, offering nothing either in the open sessions, or even the syndicate sessions.

Direct questions to the person caused obvious embarrassment and drove him even further into his shell. His skin colour changed dramatically and his breathing pattern became shorter, sharper and higher in his chest.

Over a break a conversation was started with him, indirect questions asked regarding his role, reasons for attending the course, and what would be expected of him afterwards. It transpired that he was worried about having to do appraisals for the first time, and that his credibility might be damaged.

At this point individual outcomes were agreed for him, chosen by himself. It was also agreed that the course itself was an opportunity for him to practise and develop the required skills, both through the syndicate sessions, open forums and role-plays. Again specific outcomes were agreed for the day along with appropriate tasks.

The difference in physiology, breathing rate, etc changed dramatically as the day went on, and in the mini review which took place at the end of the day, he looked and sounded completely different.

2.13 USING CONGRUENCE

Congruence is about the alignment and consistency of the message and how it is put across and received. If there is no congruence on the part of the trainer, the learners will receive mixed and different meanings. A useful way to look at it is being in rapport with oneself. This is one aspect where the trainer as role-model is key. Where walking the talk and talking the walk becomes visible and evident to the learner.

Some examples of congruence would be:

- the alignment of the message and how it is put across in terms of body language, voice, tone, language;
- the trainer as role-model;
- the alignment of beliefs and values with the message and the actions of the trainer.

USING CONGRUENCE: EXERCISES

1. Use third position to self-check for congruence.
2. Go inside and check kinesthetically (feelings, sensations and emotions). If there is a lack of alignment at some level, you will know if this is happening.
3. Practise finding a form of words, gesture, posture, etc that conveys the aligned message you wish to express.

USING CONGRUENCE: KEY POINTS

☐ Congruence is about alignment and consistency.
☐ Lack of congruence will send out mixed signals.
☐ It is about being in rapport with self.
☐ It is about aligning the message with how it is delivered, the trainer as role-model and living the beliefs.

2.14 USING ASSOCIATION/DISASSOCIATION

Association and disassociation is one part of NLP that often intrigues the newcomer, although once pointed out it is obvious and the conscious mind becomes aware of what the unconscious mind already knew.

In essence, associated means remembering something and seeing it through your own eyes. Disassociated means seeing it from somewhere else with yourself in the picture, eg as on TV or film screen.

This is a basic sub-modality (see 4.24 Using sub-modalities, page 186) division, but it is one that can make a lot of difference to the learner. Once explained many learners find that it clarifies why some parts of training have worked better for them than others, as an associated experience is more likely to be a powerful one.

Remember, also, that disassociation is an important way for the brain to distance itself from issues it doesn't relate to or want to deal with. Therefore, the skills of using disassociation can be as important as the skills of using association.

USING ASSOCIATION/DISASSOCIATION: EXERCISES

1. Review your own experiences and memories, both inside and outside training, to establish which are associated/disassociated.
2. Create associated learnings for people on key issues.
3. Ask questions of learners to establish whether they are associated/ disassociated at a particular time, eg how are they seeing this experience?
4. Use calibration skills to establish whether learners are associated/ disassociated.
5. If appropriate explain association/disassociation to learners to help them develop the skills.

USING ASSOCIATION/DISASSOCIATION: KEY POINTS

☐ Associated means seeing through own eyes.
☐ Disassociated means seeing yourself in the picture.
☐ They are basic sub-modality divisions.
☐ It helps if positive learning experiences are remembered in an associated way.
☐ It is useful to develop the skill of becoming disassociated regarding certain events.

USING ASSOCIATION/DISASSOCIATION: CASE STUDY

On an outdoor training programme designed to develop leadership skills, one person was taking control of every situation and everyone on the programme. This started to cause ripples with other participants who seemed not to know how to respond.

In reviewing a task in an open session it became apparent the individual in question was highly disassociated while reviewing and, therefore, not picking up on the effect his behaviour was causing, while the others were associated and very aware of it.

It was agreed that he develop the skills of becoming more associated, and in particular review his behaviour in the context of its impact on the other group members. He enjoyed the challenge of doing this, subsequently, literally saw himself in a new light and became a positive, purposeful leader within the group.

GETTING THE MESSAGE ACROSS

3

GETTING THE MESSAGE ACROSS

'A good listener is not just popular everywhere, but after a while they get to know something.'
Wilson Mizer

As may be inferred from the linguistic part of the title, Neuro *Linguistic* Programming (NLP) has a lot to say about language. These skills can take many forms and are very powerful for trainers to help make their training more effective. The connection between language, beliefs and values, and the non-verbal aspects of communication, helps ensure that outcomes are achieved for all concerned in the training process.

3.1 USING LANGUAGE PATTERNS

A vital skill for the effective trainer is to be able to use, recognize and respond to language patterns.

This can take a number of forms including:

- responding to questions and statements;
- matching language;
- altering states and meanings by language;
- using artfully vague language;
- recognizing belief systems revealed by language.

Responding to questions and statements

The origins for this aspect of language patterns belong to the early days of NLP originated by Bandler and Grinder and refined by a number of people since.

Bandler and Grinder developed the Meta Model which is a powerful set of language patterns that links language with the sensory experience it represents and includes key questions to clarify and specify meanings. The Meta Model is taught as part of an NLP practitioner programme.

This work is based upon ideas formulated by earlier thinkers including Chomsky who stated that language has surface structure ie the words we say, and deep structure ie the deeper and hidden meanings that represent the structure of the experience.

Using the Meta Model allows the trainer to deal with three main types of processes:

- deletion
- distortion
- generalization

It is worth pointing out that none of these are necessarily good or bad, they represent the way that people construct their models of the world. The key issue is whether these models are useful or limiting.

Deletions

There are six different ways that learners pay attention to certain parts of their experience and exclude others. The skill of identifying and challenging these can provide the missing pieces of information needed to achieve an outcome.

1. *Unspecified Nouns* – any noun that has as many meanings as there are people using that noun.
   Example: My training budget costs are up.
   Challenge: What costs specifically are up?
   Result: Recovers specific information about the noun.
2. *Unspecified Verbs* – verbs that delete something that is done.
   Example: We tried hard in that exercise.
   Challenge: How exactly did you try hard?
   Result: Recovers specific information about the experience.
3. *Nominalizations* – verbs made into nouns, thus deleting the process or action.
   Example: Education is a good thing.
   Challenge: How is education a good thing?
   Result: Turns noun back to verb and recovers the deleted process.

4. *Lack of Referential Index* – the pronoun is not specified, thus deleting to whom or what it refers.

  Example: Training is OK for some.
  Challenge: Training is OK for whom?
  Result: Recovers to whom or what 'they' refers.

5. *Comparative Deletion* – the standard of comparison is deleted.

  Example: Training is more effective.
  Challenge: More effective than what?
  Result: Recovers the standard for comparison.

6. *Lost Performative* – value judgements, rules and opinions in which the source of the assertion is missing.

  Example: There is only one right answer.
  Challenge: How do you know? or Who says...?
  Result: Recovers source of opinion or belief.

Distortions

There are three main ways to distort information. Distortion refers to things that are represented in a way that, in some way, limits the learners' ability to act and increases their potential for pain.

1. *Mind Reading* – assuming you know another person's views.

  Example: They think I am stupid.
  Challenge: How do you know?
  Or What leads you to believe that...?
  Result: Recovers source of information.

2. *Cause and Effect* – belief or implication that one person's action can cause another person's emotional reaction. There is a presupposition that people have no choice about their emotional state.

  Example: Training drives me mad.
  Challenge: How do you chose to let training drive you mad?
  Result: Recovers the imagined process of the causal connection.

3. *Pre-suppositions* – basic assumptions that must be true for a model to make sense.

  Example: He is as crazy as other trainers.
  Challenge: What leads you to believe that trainers are crazy?
  Result: Recovers the pre-supposition.

Generalizations

There are four main ways to generalize information. These generalizations define the limits of the learner's model of the world. Purposefully challenging these limits can open the doorway to new possibilities.

1. *Complex Equivalence* – where two experiences are interpreted as the same: x means y.

   Example: He went to Cambridge so he will know all about it.

   Challenge: How exactly does him going to Cambridge mean that he will know all about it?

   Result: Challenges the complex equivalence and opens up other options.

2. *Universal Quantifier* – generalizations that admit no exceptions, eg all, every, no one, always.

   Example: I will never be able to do it.

   Challenge: Never?
                Or Was there a time when you could do it?

   Result: Recovers the exceptions and counter examples.

3. *Modal Operator of Necessity* – words that imply a general rule, eg should, should not, must, must not, have to, need to, it is necessary.

   Example: You have to listen to the trainer.

   Challenge: What would happen if you did not?

   Result: Challenges the rule and explores the consequences.

4. *Modal Operator of Possibility* – words that define (to the speaker) what is possible, eg can, cannot.

   Example: I will never be able to learn the Meta Model.

   Challenge: What would happen if you could?
                Or What stops you?
                Or How do you choose not to?

   Result: Challenges the rule and explores the consequences.

All of these probably can look like a lot to bear in mind, but they are all part of the effective trainer's repertoire and, of course, only need to be used on certain occasions. Also, as with all other aspects of NLP, good trainers already use these skills elegantly and appropriately.

One thing to bear in mind with the Meta Model is how and when to use it. NLP-ers have phrases for indiscriminate use of the Meta Model, they call it Meta mayhem or Meta murder. It can only be used for maximum benefit if rapport is initially achieved and it is used sensitively and perceptively.

There is a famous story of John Grinder, co-developer of NLP, training a group in Santa Cruz in the early 1970s. Most of the class arrived the following week looking completely down and depressed. Because they had used the model indiscriminately they had alienated those people closest to them. For the trainer this is an important point to bear in mind.

It is also worth pointing out that, dependent on the content and outcomes for the training, it is possible to train learners in the skills of using the Meta Model (although this should be done in smallish chunks as it can create confusion and 'mind warp'). This can be very useful when teaching topics such as selection interviewing, appraisals, interpersonal skills, etc.

Matching language

The second skill in using language patterns is to be able to listen to, pick up on and respond to the types of words that learners use. Learners will normally reveal how they are processing information inside their head by their choice of words, eg visual, auditory, kinesthetic (touch, sensation and feelings) with some words being olfactory (smell) and gustatory (taste).

Examples of such words are listed below. In NLP these words are called 'predicates'.

Visual
Image, clear, bright, focus, glisten, glowing, eye, black, picture, colour, hazy, insight, vivid, gleam, scarce, blank, visualize, dim, dark, look, luminous, golden, perspective, vision, shine, transparent, reflect, outlook, shady, opaque, translucent.

Olfactory
Fresh, cheesy, whiff, reek, fishy, nosey, aroma, nostril, starch, bouquet, acrid, fragrant, air, rancid, stink, scent.

Auditory
Say, accent, question, click, resonate, rhythm, chatter, tinkle, hearsay, chirpy, wavelength, melody, discreet, tone, patter, harmony, drum, deaf, loud, language, monotonous, sing, clash, ring, speech, tune, scream, dumb, call, demand.

Gustatory
Flavour, sweet, appetite, sour, feed, savour, bitter, choke, gorge, spicy, chew, swallow, salt, bland, bite, juicy.

Kinesthetic
Weight, move, smooth, handle, loose, thrust, texture, grasp, warm, touch, lift, pushy, rub, tight, contact, sticky, solid, tackle, cold, itch, pressure, rough, insensitive, flow, firm, turn, uptight, tickle, shrug.

Non-sensory-based words
Remember, workout, know, sense, think, recognize, attend, understand, notice, decide, explain, arrange, perceive.

By paying careful attention to learners' words when they are making a point, it is possible to enhance their learning by matching their language in the response. Equally, if appropriate, mismatching by deliberately responding in a different system can be a very elegant way of choosing not to agree. It is also possible to pace and lead with language in exactly the same way as with non-verbal communication ie create rapport, recognize by a physiological, verbal or other signal that you have created rapport, then lead into another language system. Most learners will have a preferred language system and allowing them to create greater flexibility in their thinking, learning and communication skills is a very powerful tool for a trainer.

Altering states and meanings by language

One specific use of language patterns to alter states and meanings is the Meta Model. Any point made that is a Meta Model violation and is therefore challenged by a trainer will create change in the learner. The skill is ensuring that the change is a purposeful one and not one that compounds a disempowering belief, a stuck state or a negative answer. Some examples are:

Learner: I'll never get the hang of this.
Trainer: Never? *Or* 'What would happen if you could'?

Learner: This subject is difficult.
Trainer: Which specific part of this subject is difficult?

Learner: Everyone else is cleverer than me.
Trainer: In what specific way is everyone cleverer than you?

Obviously none of these challenges stand alone. It will probably be necessary to follow up one challenge with another in order to move the learner in a different direction. The individual and group dynamics can be altered dramatically by supportive, rapport-based use of these forms of language. In addition individuals and groups will assimilate these patterns unconsciously and you will hear the quality of the language and its impact change dramatically, even over a coffee break or lunch.

Because most learners start from the premise that either learning can only be one way, eg hard and dull, or have fixed beliefs regarding themselves and their abilities it is important that care is taken with this process. Some individuals, often the visuals, break out very quickly and visible change will occur. Others, often the kinesthetics, will take a lot longer but the change will be deep and profound. The auditory learner may well give less obvious evidence of altered states so very careful attention needs to be paid to anything different in their choice of words, physiology, eye accessing cues, etc.

Using artfully vague language

The Meta Model is a very powerful aid to the trainer and will achieve profound results, but, on occasions, its use will not be appropriate. Also there is a balance between using it effectively and over using it. The ability to use artfully vague language instead of, or as well as, the Meta Model equips the trainer with an all-round armoury of skills.

The recognition of the use of artfully vague language came to the fore in the 1970s with work carried out analysing the skills of Milton Ericson, the world famous hypnotherapist. Ericson was the original president of the American Society for Clinical Hypnosis and had a reputation for achieving results that no one else could and for being the most sensitive person in the field to minor changes in behaviour. One of his key skills was the way he induced and utilized trance states, so allowing individuals to find their own resources to overcome problem issues. He was one of the key people that Bandler and Grinder modelled when carrying out the early work that was developed into NLP.

He had a very strong conviction that too much intervention could produce poor quality or short-term results and that the only way to achieve long-term, purposeful change was to build on or develop the skills of the individual. Many trainers would recognize this as a belief of their own.

The advantage of what became known as the Milton model is that it builds upon the natural resources of the individual and allows their mind to work naturally and in a motivated way. His technique was based on the belief that the unconscious mind had a positive intention for everything, including what might, at the time, appear to be the oddest behaviour. He also believed that individuals made the best choice available to them at a particular time and that, at some level, individuals were already equipped with the necessary resources to make effective changes. He saw his role as allowing the individual to get to those resources.

The key, therefore, to being really effective for Ericson was to meet the individual at *their own level*, rather than impose conditions and restraints on them externally. This meant not looking for, or imposing, logic but rather to look for the purpose behind any action.

Putting this into practice for a trainer can, oddly enough, mean doing less to achieve more. For example, when being asked a particularly hostile or probing question it can be very easy to become defensive or to become too strident or strong in the response, and lose the group being worked with. Equally, in dealing with an indifferent individual or group it can be very easy to 'over communicate' or 'overload' in an effort to cause a reaction or make something happen.

The use of artfully vague language, or ambiguity as some people call it, bypasses the searching spotlight of the logical conscious mind and draws out the specific needs the individual has, rather than impose them from the outside. For example:

'And you can find those resources that help you in those ways that you want them to, even the ones you are not necessarily aware of yet...'

This puts the learner into a state known as 'downtime'. Downtime is the process of going inside to find meaning rather than taking meaning from external stimuli. Day dreaming is one form of downtime and 'day dreaming with a purpose' is a very effective way of developing new approaches. Very popular in the USA, although not normally used by trainers in the UK, is the 'guided fantasy' technique, which engages both the conscious and unconscious mind in order to create new options.

In putting learners into a 'downtime' state the trainer is actually using the opposite of the Meta Model, ie deliberately using deletions, distortions and generalizations. This puts the learner in the position of having to complete the picture and put their own meaning into the situation.

One step on from this is deliberately not supplying all the information so that the conscious mind is kept busy filling in the missing pieces. This means that the unconscious can get on with the job of attaching meaning, finding resources without the 'interference' of the conscious mind. In other words, getting directly to the intuitive, creative part of the brain.

A number of trainers might feel uncomfortable with this as it might seem too imprecise and out of control. If that is the case it is worth remembering that the trainer should be prepared to use anything that helps the learner. On occasions, this may mean trainers having to develop their own skill range and/or extend their own comfort zones. Yet most people use artfully vague language all the time, with their partner, their children, friends, colleagues, etc. Certainly a great deal of 'normal' communication takes place this way, and it should be part of the repertoire of any effective trainer.

One other point that is also important to consider is that to many learners the trainer is an example of 'best practice'. Therefore, having the skill and flexibility to use whatever is appropriate is a very visible demonstration of this.

Recognizing belief systems revealed by language

The language used by a learner will be a very strong indication of the belief system that lies beneath at a deep structure level. The comment 'I have never been any good at this subject', although committing a Meta Model violation, is very revealing of a deep-rooted belief system. Other examples while being less overtly individual, eg 'That will never work here', are equally revealing.

A key issue is that the beliefs that learners have impact on what and how they learn. Those who have the expectation that they can learn a topic or skill, or will have future success, tend to achieve their expectation. There are two types of what are called 'personal agency beliefs':

- capability beliefs – 'I think I can handle this subject';
- context beliefs – 'I am so busy at work it is harder to find time for learning'.

The problem is that the trainer may not know how to operate for an individual or a group. Therefore, there is a need to pay close attention to language as well as non-verbal communication to spot the clues.

Eric Jensen in his book *The Learning Brain* quotes the long-term study carried out by researchers on 250 students aged 12–15. In this study it was found that the single best advance prediction of success in mathematics was *their expectancy* of future maths success.

The implications for the trainer are twofold. One, it is vital for the trainer to have high expectations that are conveyed to the group; language such as 'I know some of you are going to find this difficult' will indicate a strong trainer belief and anchor it negatively in the group. Secondly, picking up on language patterns as evidence of disempowering beliefs in individuals and groups and developing 'controllable short-term goals' with them is one way of handling negative belief systems.

One other aspect of recognizing language patterns to reveal belief systems is, if a disempowering belief is revealed, to use language skills to help the learner redress it. An example would be:

Trainer: What stops you from learning that?
Learner: I can't learn it because of X.
Trainer: How is that a problem?
Learner: I feel stupid when it happens.
Trainer: How do you know to feel stupid?
            What makes you feel stupid?
            When do you feel stupid?
Learner: X happens and I feel stupid.
Trainer: What does X mean, that it makes you feel stupid?
            How is it possible that X makes you feel stupid instead of bright and creative?

For further aspects of, and techniques for dealing with these issues, all the topics in this section are useful.

USING LANGUAGE PATTERNS: EXERCISES

Meta Model

1. Use the Meta Model, practise looking for and responding to specific violations.
2. Listen for Meta Model violations even if you choose not to challenge them.
3. Use the Meta Model to help learners (and yourself) to clarify outcomes.

Matching language

1. Listen for representation systems and predicates used by learners. Match their language pattern by responding in the same pattern (but using different words).
2. Practise cross-over mirroring using language, ie listen to their language, match it by your voice tone, tempo, etc.

Altering states and meanings

1. Use the Meta Model process.
2. Use language to achieve change – watch for language, non-verbals, eye accessing cue responses.
3. Practise daily 1 and 2 in different ways with learners with either a visual, auditory or kinesthetic preference.

Using artfully vague language

1. Practise talking to the unconscious mind before (or instead of) the conscious mind.
2. Use language that puts learners into 'downtime' (before then, of course, bringing them back into 'uptime').

Recognizing belief systems revealed by language

1. Listen for belief systems being revealed.
2. Ask specific questions to get to belief systems.
3. Practise carrying positive beliefs regarding learners and their capabilities, watch the effect this has when running training programmes.

USING LANGUAGE PATTERNS: KEY POINTS

☐ Be aware of use for:
  - responding to questions and statements;
  - matching language;
  - altering states and meanings by language;
  - using artfully vague language;
  - recognizing belief systems revealed by language.

- ☐ Use the Meta Model to deal with:
  - – deletions;
  - – distortions;
  - – generalizations.
- ☐ Use matching language to create rapport with learners.
- ☐ Mismatch language to break rapport, if appropriate.
- ☐ Lead by using language.
- ☐ Use language to alter states and meanings.
- ☐ Use artfully vague language.
- ☐ Recognize belief systems revealed by language.
- ☐ Pay great attention to all the complexities and subtleties of the learners' language.

USING LANGUAGE PATTERNS: CASE STUDY

A training programme was being designed in conjunction with a HR manager and a group of line managers. The purpose of the programme was to develop an empowered team culture.

During the discussions to plan the programme it became obvious from the language patterns used by the managers involved that different people had different beliefs regarding the end product of the training and what it could achieve.

Some of the managers were using lack of referential index phrases like 'that programme will only be OK for some'; others were using nominalizations like 'empowerment must be good for all concerned'. Another group used universal quantifiers about the programme 'never being able to change anything'.

Through a combination of Meta Model questions, matching language and recognizing belief systems revealed by language, agreement was reached on what could usefully be achieved.

3.2 USING METAPHORS

Metaphors are used in all walks of life from childhood fairy stories, where good triumphs over evil – a frog becomes a prince, all the way through to business where evoking warlike states and 'rallying the troops' are used all the time. Many day-to-day sayings are simple metaphors and are readily accepted by large numbers of people, where the real point or a more complex use of language would actually complicate or alienate.

Examples of simple metaphors, also fitted within representation systems, are:

Visual metaphors

I see what you mean.
He looked crazy.
Try to see things my way.
It is one of my most vivid memories.
I have a vision of how things could be.
You have to recognize their point of view.
Things are looking up.
I can see right through him.
I want a different perspective.
Shed some light on the matter.
He is making a spectacle of himself.
She is the image of her mother.
Let us look on the bright side.
He has a blind spot.

The outlook is dim.
Show me what you mean.
Clear as mud.
Seeing eye to eye.

I am trying to picture it.

Let us look at this closely.

It appears that... view.
Crystal clear.
Things look black for him.
Turn a blind eye.
I've got a hazy idea.

It's not really clear.
It's a crazy scene.
Silver lining.

Auditory metaphors

We are on the same wavelength.
Speaking the same language.
Tune into this.
The accent on success.
Mind your Ps and Qs.
I like your story.
With a song in my heart.
Music in my ears.
A ding-dong row.
He's drummed it into her.
Lost for words.
I hear what you are saying.

Quiet as a mouse.
Sounds good.
Tone it down.
Living in harmony.
Talking gobbledegook.
Rings a bell.
Turn a deaf ear.
Struck dumb.
Calling the tune.
Shouting the odds.
Strikes a chord.
Noise in the system.

Kinesthetic metaphors

I'm ready to tackle this head-on.
I've got a feel for the place.
Maintaining a sense of balance.
Get a grip on yourself.
She is as solid as a rock.
He's a wet blanket.
His feelings were hurt.
A sticky situation.

Pull yourself together.
Hot headed.
Can you grasp the idea?
He rubs me up the wrong way.
Scratch that idea.
One step at a time.
A pat on the back.
Hold on a minute.

He wants something concrete.	Get a grip on yourself.
A cool customer.	I feel it in my bones.
I need a hand.	Things just flowed.

Using more complex metaphors allows the unconscious mind to search meaning and resources for itself. Therefore, in order to create a purposeful metaphor that will move towards solving a problem or issue, the relationships between the parts of the story must be the same as the relationships between the elements of the problem.

One exercise often used in training courses where participants are dealing with difficult personal issues is:

1. A tells B about a current problem.
2. B listens, notes the key elements of the problem and the language used (as well as physiology, eye accessing cues) etc.
3. B then creates a story which represents this, building in the key elements in the same sequence, using matching language, up to the point that A had finished stating the problem.
4. B tells A the story. At the point of the story where the problem has been specified, B stops, A takes over and finishes the story.

Note: It is not the role of B to offer a solution. The metaphor used should be picked up on and completed by A.

This is obviously a structured experience and yet time and again it allows A to find something useful in themselves that they were unaware of before the process started. Feedback indicates that because A has not been 'sold' a solution and because it is self-created there is greater chance of implementation and success.

The key steps in building metaphors are:

(a) Gather information.
(b) Build the metaphor:
   - select context;
   - be aware of strategy used;
   - reframe the original problem.
(c) Tell it:
   - be sensitive and aware of other person;
   - be elegant in use of situations.
(d) Wait for a response:
   - allow them to find own solution;
   - pick up on non-verbal communication signals.

Within the skills required by the trainer there is the recognition of the two most useful types of metaphor:

- isomorphic;
- elicitation.

An *isomorphic metaphor* parallels a story of a learner at a formal level. The key skills are pacing and leading, gaining access to conscious and unconscious resources, creation of a range of solutions that allows the learner to choose from a number of possible solutions.

An *elicitation metaphor* on the other hand, is designed to create a specific response. This means getting to a variety of states of consciousness and the resources that go with them. This aids learners to achieve wider access to their own resources, creates more possible solutions and makes more choices available.

In the book *Maps, Models and the Structure of Reality*, (Kim Kostere and Linda Malatesta, 1990), from which these two definitions are taken, the writers state that 'there are two concepts that are central to understanding metaphor:

- displaced referential index;
- transderivational search'.

They then go on to explain each concept.

Displaced referential index refers to the 'as if' quality that exists in all metaphors. Within each metaphor there is a certain element of symbolism. The symbolism can be either abstract or concrete. Metaphors that contain abstract symbolism are known as deep metaphors. Those containing symbolism that is more concrete are called shallow metaphors. In either case, the learner will usually identify with one or more of the symbols in the story and, from that perspective, interpret and internalize its meaning.

Transderivational search is the means by which language is connected to experience. It is via the process of transderivational search that the learner associates the words used in the metaphor to his/her own model of the world. Thus each learner's interpretation of the metaphor will be unique because the words used in the story become associated to his/her personal internal sensory systems. It is our belief that each learner interprets the presented metaphor in the way that is most congruent with his/her own being and in accordance with the desired goal.

All of this potentially complicates what should be a straightforward skill for the trainer, but it does illustrate the levels that these skills can be taken to.

A well-known NLP story which illustrates some of the issues that trainers/teachers face is as follows:

One dark evening as a farmer passed a well he heard a cry for help from its depths. 'What is happening?' he yelled down. A voice replied 'I am a teacher and I have accidentally fallen into this well and am unable to free myself.' 'Keep cool and I will fetch a rope or ladder,' responded the farmer. 'Just a moment please,' said the teacher. 'Your grammar and diction need to be improved, kindly make the necessary changes.' 'If that is what seems important to you,' angrily stated the farmer, 'then I suggest you stay where you are until I learn to speak correctly.' And he proceeded on his way.

This story will affect different people in different ways and each individual, based on their beliefs and model of the world, will assign different meanings to it. Teachers may well find it unfair and scurrilous regarding them, but recognize something in other teachers. Learners will probably enjoy it for a variety of reasons.

Using metaphors en masse in a group is a fair and creative way to stimulate creativity, problem solving and create new thoughts and perceptions. Getting small groups to develop metaphors for the following examples is one way to start.

Learning is like a growing tree.
Man is on top of the mountain of life.
A rucksack can be full of stones or dreams.
Life is like a merry go round.
Learning is a marathon.

Metaphors work on a number of levels. The main reason being that although there is a deep structure beneath them, which it is useful to know and understand, they can be used conversationally all of the time, and, used elegantly, they will achieve important shifts for learners, probably without them realizing it.

Two final thoughts for trainers who may be wondering whether metaphors are really as powerful and useful as have been described. One, Jesus based a lot of his teachings on some form of metaphor. Two, being a trainer is actually a metaphor for life with beliefs about what can be achieved.

USING METAPHORS: EXERCISES

1. Use exercise covered in this section.
2. Use skills of exercise in and outside training area, measure effectiveness by response and level of change and learning.
3. Use the skills of building metaphors.
4. Get learners to use metaphors on each other (and on you).
5. Listen for metaphors, probably used unconsciously, inside and outside the training context.

USING METAPHORS: KEY POINTS

☐ Be aware of own and learners' metaphors.
☐ Use metaphors to help learning be more effective.
☐ Help learners create their own metaphors.
☐ Follow steps for creating metaphors:
  – gather information;
  – build the metaphor;
  – tell it;
  – wait for a response.
☐ Be aware of two types of metaphor:
  – isomorphic;
  – elicitation.
☐ Be aware of two concepts for understanding metaphors:
  – displaced referential index;
  – transderivational search.
☐ Use metaphors to stimulate creativity, problem solve and create new thoughts and perceptions.
☐ Develop own metaphors for training, specific materials and issues.

3.3 USING REFRAMING

Like metaphors reframing is a simple but powerful tool within the trainer's toolkit. Reframing can be defined as *changing the way of understanding a statement or behaviour to give it another meaning.*

In training this can be very important as learners can be very quick to attach meaning to certain words and situations, eg I get very nervous at the thought of a presentation/an interview, and this can inhibit their effectiveness.

There are two main types of reframe – context and content.

Context reframes
Virtually all human behaviour is useful in some context. For example, falling asleep in meetings is not considered useful, but being able to fall asleep on going to bed is. Presenting information in a very detailed manner for a written report may be very useful, but being that detailed in telling a child why they should do as they are told will not be as effective – they will lose interest in the key point very quickly.

Content reframes
The content is the specific main part the learner chooses to focus on. Most people have an awareness of content reframing via politics and advertising. Both of these take specific parts of the content, eg a Cabinet minister speaking out against party policy is shown as the Government

encouraging people to have their own opinions. In advertising, for example, driving a particular car means that you are stylish, using this product means that you care about your family. In all these cases one specific aspect is focused on to create wider and possibly different interpretations.

Listening closely to the language learners use will give an insight into their beliefs and give the opportunity for a reframe. Most reframes can be achieved by Meta Model and sleight of mouth patterns (see 3.5 Using sleight of mouth, page 87). The purpose is to shift the disempowering belief/negative view and put it into a different light. It is not to gild the lily and pretend that everything is OK when it is not. It is one more way to open out the learner to new thoughts, ideas, opportunities and actions.

As a flexible trainer, therefore, rather than just repeating a process, which on this particular occasion is not working, or not working as well as usual, try something different, not only in terms of content but also style and approach. To quote Eric Jensen (1994a) 'if you are teaching a class and having difficulty explaining something, try a different approach. How would a blind person do it, how would a deaf person explain it? How would a foreigner explain it? What about a handicapped person, an athlete or a movie star?'

USING REFRAMING: EXERCISES

1. Get learners (and self) to follow this process:
    (a) Think of an aspect of learning that they see as a problem.
    (b) Get them to complete the following sentences:
        − It's difficult for me to...
        − I hope that...
        − If I... then...
        − I'm going to try to...
        − I can't...
    (c) Reflect and review on (b).
    (d) Rewrite the sentences, changing to:
        − It's a challenge for me to...
        − I trust that...
        − When I... then...
        − I'm going to...
        − I will (or I can)...
    (e) Check which process changes perceptions and creates a more positive view.
    (f) Put the new situation into an outcome, if helpful.
    (g) Anchor, if helpful.
    (h) Future pace, if helpful.
    (i) Be aware of physiological shifts.

2. Practise getting learners to follow this process:
   (a) Working with a partner; tell your partner how bad you are at some aspect of learning, eg being good with numbers, go into the full gory difficulty of it all.
   (b) After two minutes your partner does the same (avoid anchoring this in any way).
   (c) Clear your mind, take a deep breath, then take two minutes *convincing* your partner of a complete change, that you can now do the aspect of learning, be aware of your language, physiology, feelings, etc.
   (d) After two minutes it's your partner's turn.
   (e) Set an outcome, if helpful.
   (f) Anchor, if helpful.
   (g) Future pace, if helpful.

USING REFRAMING: KEY POINTS

☐ Use reframes to change understanding or behaviour or give it another meaning.
☐ Use context and content reframes.
☐ Use Meta Model.
☐ Use sleight of mouth patterns.
☐ Always be prepared to try something different.

USING REFRAMING: CASE STUDY

A learner on a training course continually put himself down regarding his ability to learn the subject being taught. This was in complete contradiction to the evidence and the feedback of other course members.

It came to the point that the group, while generally trying hard to help, were actually embedding a negative anchor. At this point the group decided to change its strategy.

During the next exercise, rather than give feedback on performance, they discussed the variety of situations (ie contexts) the skills could be applied to, asking the individual for his view. Repeating this process throughout the afternoon resulted in, during the review at the end of the day, the learner putting forward six examples of how he would be able to use the skills back at work.

3.4 USING BACKTRACKING

Backtracking is like summarizing but involves using the exact words that the learner has used. Summarizing is a very important skill to have and one aspect of that skill is interpreting precisely the meaning of the words used by the learner.

The skill of backtracking as against summarizing is to use the actual words rather than your version of them. This is not quite as easy as it sounds as, particularly in the UK, it can feel odd and sometimes sound as though you are stupid or being sarcastic with the learner. Therefore, the voice tone and emphasis used is critical. This is where the skills of NLP can be so useful.

It is particularly useful where the trainer is trying to achieve a level of agreement with a learner, or there is an argument going on, or the trainer is being attacked or belittled, or the learner is being particularly hesitant or nervous in expressing a view.

An example of a difficult situation would be:

Learner: You are always racing ahead before I have fully understood what is being said.
Trainer: You say that I am always racing ahead before you have fully understood what is being said.

or

Learner: You overcomplicate everything you say.
Trainer: You say that I overcomplicate everything I say.

At this point if the learner has been aggressive the heat is taken out of the situation because they have to agree with the trainer or repeat the point or make another point – at which point the trainer should repeat the backtrack on the new point.

It is vital that the trainer backtracks literally as this is assertive behaviour against the aggression or passiveness of the learner and creates new opportunities, due to the trainer not getting drawn into the situation. It would also be possible to use the Meta Model, but the trainer would need to make a judgement as to which technique would be most appropriate to the circumstances.

Having achieved a level of rapport and common ground the trainer can then move forward in a more positive direction. This can take the form of:

(a) Seeking ideas/direction from the learner. This should be future based to avoid repeating the quicksand of the past.
(b) Agree to come back to the issue later with both parties committing to coming back with solutions.

(c) The trainer can ask the relevancy question, ie what does X have to do with Y? (X being the comment, Y being the purpose of the learning.)
(d) The trainer can ask a spotlight question ie when you say X, what are you really trying to say?
(e) The trainer can offer ideas and direction of their own based upon the backtracked comments of the learner.

The key point regarding backtracking is that it is very hard for a learner to stay aggressive or passive if the backtrack has been calmly, assertively and accurately carried out. The only thing they might object to is the backtrack itself, so voice tonality and non-verbal communication need to be appropriate as well.

Backtracking is one of those techniques that sounds simple and straightforward and turns out not to be in practice. Like all of the techniques put forward in this section it requires skill and judgement as to when, and to what extent, to use it. Used appropriately it purposefully changes the dynamics of a particular situation, but it will require the use of a range of NLP skills, eg creating rapport, maintaining a positive personal state, non-verbal communication, for it to be used effectively.

USING BACKTRACKING: EXERCISES

1. Backtrack wherever you are not sure of a learner's true statement or question.
2. Practise shorter or longer backtracks dependent on your view of the type of learner you are dealing with.
3. Backtrack on days (sessions), training, activities/outcomes.
4. Ask people to backtrack you.

USING BACKTRACKING: KEY POINTS

☐ Repeat back *exactly* what has been said.
☐ Stay positive, focused and assertive.
☐ Use appropriate voice tone and non-verbal communication.
☐ Having backtracked, move to a more positive direction.
 – Seek ideas direction.
 – Agree to come back to issue later.
 – Ask a relevancy question.
 – Ask a spotlight question.
 – Move in a forward direction.
 – Use the appropriate NLP skills.

3.5 USING SLEIGHT OF MOUTH

These sleight of mouth skills are based upon the work carried out by the American, Robert Dilts. As part of the work undertaken in developing Neuro Linguistic Programming, Dilts became aware of the wide variety of meanings that could be attributed to certain words and phrases. It was also clear from analysing the key skills of highly effective communicators that they were able, either consciously or unconsciously, to use these skills to bring about changes in people and situations.

The other interesting point about sleight of mouth is that, used effectively, it can, like reframing and metaphors, actually shift a belief about a particular topic.

Listed below are the 14 classic Robert Dilts sleight of mouth definitions. Later in this section we put them into a trainer and learner context.

Redefine: substituting a new word for one of the words used in the belief statement that means something similar but has different implications.

Consequence: directing attention to an effect (positive or negative) of the belief or the relationship defined by the belief.

Intention: directing attention to the purpose or intention of the belief (positive or negative).

Chunk down: breaking the elements of the belief into small enough pieces that it changes the relationship defined by the belief.

Chunk up: generalizing an element of the belief to a larger classification that changes the relationship defined by the belief.

Counter example: finding an example that does not fit.

Another outcome: challenging the relevance of the belief and switching to another issue altogether.

Analogy: finding a relationship analogous to that defined by the belief, but which has different implications.

Apply to self: evaluating the belief statement itself according to the relationship or criteria defined by the belief.

Hierarchy of criteria: re-evaluating the belief according to a criterion that is more important than any addressed by the belief.

Change frame size: re-evaluating the implication of the belief in the context of a larger (or shorter) time, frame, a larger number of people (or from an individual point of view) or a bigger or smaller perspective.

Meta frame: evaluating the belief from the frame of an ongoing, personally oriented context ie establishing a belief about the belief.

Model of the world: re-evaluating the belief from the framework of a different model of the world.

Reality strategy: re-evaluating the belief accounting for the fact that people operate from cognitive perceptions of the world to build beliefs.

Just listing the definitions as has been done above can be a fairly intimidating process. Most trainers, on reading them, will recognize some of their potential uses and also realize that they already use a number of them. As ever the key judgement and skill is in using the right one at the right time, although in fact using the wrong one can sometimes shift things in a useful and purposeful way.

An example of a typical learner comment and the various sleight of mouth options is listed below.

Learner comment
Learning this subject is too difficult.

Trainer sleight of mouth response
Redefine: It is not difficult by itself, it can be easy and fun if you want it to be.
Consequence: Beliefs like this become self-fulfilling prophecies because they stop you exploring other options.
Intention: I know your intention is to prevent false hope that learning can be easy but you are preventing any chance of this.
Chunk down: What particular (specific) aspect of learning is difficult?
Chunk up: Does that mean that all learning in life is difficult?
Counter example: There are many examples of learning where it can be easy; *or* Difficulties can affect all aspects of life.
Another outcome: The issue is not that learning this subject is difficult but rather what makes life fun, enjoyable and easy.
Analogy: Learning is like the sun's rays, it can be easy to absorb and soak up and achieve a nice tan and change, but if it is overdone or not approached properly it can be difficult and hard work. It, therefore, requires thought and a positive plan to make it work.
Apply to self: That is a disempowering belief to hold on to too strongly.
Hierarchy of criteria: Do you not think it is more important to focus on the positive side of life rather than just a small part?
Change frame size: Is this a belief that you would like your son/ daughter to have? *or* If everyone had that belief no one would ever learn anything.
Meta frame: You only believe that because you do not have a model of life that allows you to explore, track and test all the complex variables that contribute to the learning process.
Model of the world: Many trainers believe that learning in life is a complex process with many ups and downs, but that those people who enjoy most parts of it achieve a greater sense of contribution and self-worth.
Reality strategy: How would you know if that point was not true?

If faced with the particular comment 'learning this subject is too difficult' many trainers' strategy would be to either ignore or challenge the observation. Either of these strategies may be absolutely appropriate, it is not a question of right or wrong; it is about having sufficient choice, and the flexibility of trainer behaviour to respond in the most effective, purposeful manner. Equally, not all of the sleight of mouth responses would be appropriate, but a lot of trainers would equally find a tendency to respond in a predictable, patterned way to comments and situations created by the learners.

USING SLEIGHT OF MOUTH: EXERCISES

1. Practise specific sleight of mouth patterns.
2. Listen out for how learners use sleight of mouth (even if they have never heard of it).
3. Use new, unusual sleight of mouth patterns with learners, watch and listen for the response.
4. Get an individual to state a problem, then *other* group members apply sleight of mouth patterns to it.

USING SLEIGHT OF MOUTH: KEY POINTS

☐ People attribute a wide variety of meanings to certain words and phrases.
☐ Using sleight of mouth can shift beliefs.
☐ There are 14 sleight of mouth categories that can be used:
  - redefine
  - consequence
  - intention
  - chunk down
  - chunk up
  - counter example
  - another outcome
  - analogy
  - apply to self
  - hierarchy of criteria
  - change frame size
  - meta frame
  - model of the world
  - reality strategy.

USING SLEIGHT OF MOUTH: CASE STUDY

A discussion was taking place on a training course in which two people were arguing about the validity of a particular technique and its relevance back at work. As the argument went on each learner became more locked into their point of view. Without specifically mentioning sleight of mouth, the trainer asked each learner to:

(a) think of six different ways of regarding the issue; and
(b) three different ways someone they knew might approach the situation.

The outcome of this was that within five minutes a different, wider view was agreed, and the course moved on.

3.6 USING QUOTES

Virtually all trainers have their own stock selection of jokes, anecdotes and stories, and are able to use them with skill and ease to match or create a particular situation. Quotes also fall into this category and are extremely useful in aiding or shifting the dynamics of a group or helping to embed a specific point. All key aspects of the NLP repertoire.

Traditionally most quotes have come from literature, plays and famous people from history, Shakespeare, Oscar Wilde, Abraham Lincoln, being obvious choices. Nowadays while these and others are still quoted, it is as likely to be a modern management guru such as Tom Peters, Kenneth Blanchard, Lea Iacocca, Warren Bennis, Stephen Covey.

This, therefore, gives the trainer the opportunity to widen the menu of choice while also giving proven evidence to the audience of being up to date and on the ball.

USING QUOTES: EXERCISES

1. Read books of quotes, think of specific linkages to training, use the quotes, gather feedback using sensory activity, listening skills, etc.
2. Ask other people for their favourite quotes.
3. Use NLP sensory skills to establish what works, for whom, and in what circumstances.

USING QUOTES: KEY POINTS

- ☐ Use quotes to shift group dynamics, emphasize a point.
- ☐ Be aware, using NLP techniques, of what works, what effect is being caused.
- ☐ Stay up to date with your quotes.

3.7 USING EMBEDDED COMMANDS

This skill is very important for the effective trainer as it helps ensure that training sessions are dynamic and achieve maximum benefit for learners.

Most people who have attended training courses will recognize the trainer who either apologizes in advance, eg 'I know you don't want to be here, but' or 'I know you won't like this subject, but'; or alternatively acts with arrogance and condescension, eg 'I realize you will never know as much as me on this subject' or 'This is very difficult but don't worry I'm here to help'.

The effect this has on a group is normally visible to all concerned, except possibly the trainer, and shows very little respect and recognition of the learners' needs. Using positive embedded commands allows the trainer to work with the best interests of the group and allows 'milestones' to summarize key learnings.

Embedded commands should always have a positive intention and normally be interspersed in the middle of conversations or input, eg 'By the time we will have finished this session *you will have the full knowledge of...*'. These should also be anchored by either voice tonality and/or spatial anchoring to achieve maximum benefit.

The underlying purpose in using embedded commands is to prepare the unconscious mind for events and learnings *before* making it explicit to the conscious mind. This allows the conscious mind to pre-prepare itself and helps ensure that the full learning is accessed. It is also worthwhile repeating key embedded suggestions at the end of a particular session to make it clear what the key learnings have been.

In using embedded commands the learner is not consciously aware of the positive language being used. This means that, although they don't know when or how, they feel more confident, relaxed and comfortable about the situation and/or the learnings.

The story or language around the embedded commands may not be particularly important and in fact may on occasions deliberately distract or allow the mind to wander, but it does allow for the embedding to take place. Naturally this technique should be used appropriately and match the needs and current situation of the learning group and the individual in it.

This technique can be used in a variety of ways, such as getting them to do something while embedding commands related to something else, eg 'while you achieve good results on this subject remember we have another valuable topic coming up after lunch'. The conscious mind of the learner will focus on the here and now, while the unconscious mind will pick up on the message embedded for later in the day.

USING EMBEDDED COMMANDS: EXERCISES

1. Use affirmations on self/learners.
2. Use voice tonality to anchor embedded commands.
3. Try using embedded commands using different, or a mix of, representation systems.
4. Repeat embedded commands at key points, including the end.

USING EMBEDDED COMMANDS: KEY POINTS

☐ Use embedded commands to prepare for later learning, both inside and outside the learning event.
☐ Repeat embedded commands at end of a session to re-emphasize learnings.
☐ Stay constantly alert to the appropriate use of embedded commands.

USING EMBEDDED COMMANDS: CASE STUDY

A situation had developed on a training course where the manager of the participants had decided to join in for part of the course. This resulted in a partial hijacking of the programme and movement away from the original objectives, to the obvious consternation of the participants.

The trainer's response was to use a *repeated* series of embedded commands, eg 'at the point we reach this issue on the programme *you will be able to visualize where these skills fit*, and how they will achieve the department's vision'.

Another example was 'everyone has a view on how best to see this through and *it will become clearer when we get there*'. This combined not just embedded commands anchored in voice and spatially. It also recognized that the manager's language was predominantly visual and matched him at that level.

The manager quite happily sat back at this stage, listened to the input and the group discussion, and commented afterwards on how useful he had found the whole process.

Another simple example is quoted later in this book (page 114). When introducing a video on a training programme try saying 'you can all sit back now and enjoy this video prior to us *putting it into action afterwards*'. Then follow it through with the appropriate actions.

3.8 USING RELEVANCY CHALLENGES

There are a number of situations where it can be useful to use a relevancy challenge. For example, if someone in a group is playing games and trying to put you down by using sarcasm, rather than confront them on a personal level, which almost certainly will create an aggressive/defensive/polarity reaction, it is better not to respond to their overt verbal assault but to dig beneath to find their real question, if it exists. This can also fit in with the use of backtracking (see 3.4 Using backtracking, page 85). It also requires the full range of NLP skills eg calibration, congruency, creating rapport, language patterns, to ensure that the technique is carried out with integrity and harmony.

Two examples of relevancy questions:

What does that (their comment) have to do with this (the purpose of the training)?
or
When you ask that (their comment) what are you really trying to say?

Having got a response, probe and clarify, using non-threatening questions to help the other person express their full point. Then, again neutrally, respond to the point and move on. All of this needs to be done in an assertive, non-threatening voice tone with a suitably congruent body position.

Normally it is better to avoid 'why' questions as these can drive the questioner into defence or justification of the question or their reasons for asking for it.

With someone who is very hesitant and having trouble articulating their question the relevancy questions are also very useful. It is normally best to avoid, except in exceptional circumstances, trying to 'mind read' the questioner. It shows more respect for the individual and the quality of their question to help them to express it for themselves.

USING RELEVANCY CHALLENGES: EXERCISES

1. Use the two relevancy questions covered in this section.
2. Practise using appropriate voice tone, language patterns, calibration, etc.

USING RELEVANCY CHALLENGES: KEY POINTS

☐ Use to avoid getting into aggressive/defensive situations.
☐ Get to the real point behind their response.
☐ Use the two relevancy questions:
  – What does that have to do with (this)?
  – When you ask (that) what are you really trying to say?
☐ Probe and clarify.
☐ Keep voice tone and non-verbal communication assertive and neutral.
☐ Avoid 'why' questions.
☐ Also use with hesitant/shy learners.
☐ Avoid 'mind reading'.
☐ Show total respect for the learner.

USING RELEVANCY CHALLENGES: CASE STUDY

A particularly belligerent manager was disagreeing with the points the trainer was putting across. As the manager continued to press his point the trainer almost fell into the trap of responding as if she herself were being attacked.

In using calibration skills and listening to the voice tone of the manager, it was apparent that he was playing to the audience, and straying further and further from the real issue being discussed.

When the manager said that he didn't think the trainer had ever run a business and didn't understand the real world, it would have been easy to take the comment personally, thus playing into the manager's hands. Therefore, rather than do that, the trainer's response was, 'What does not having run a business have to do with developing an effective team briefing structure for your department?' The manager's response, calibrated by the trainer, was that they were two different things. The trainer then asked the manager what his objectives were for wanting team briefing and the conversation moved on.

3.9 GATHERING INFORMATION

Sometimes trainers, like some presenters we have all seen, become so caught up in how it is working for them, that they lose contact with the audience and miss out on all signals and information available. This can create confusion in the learners and make it harder for them to obtain maximum benefit from the training.

Rooted at the heart of NLP is the belief that everybody creates their own perception or model of the world. Our internal experience interacts all the time with the external or sensory experience. The purpose of the information gathering model is to use linguistic information gathering techniques to help learners reconnect their sensory experiences with their language.

This technique involves asking questions (as in the Meta Model) to uncover unspecified nouns, unspecified verbs, universal quantifiers, modal operators of possibility and necessity, nominalizations and causes and effect. It has three main uses:

- by itself as a separate set of tools;
- as part of the identification outcome frame;
- as part of the adding resource frame.

We have already covered these techniques (see 3.1 Using language patterns, page 67). However a quick revisit at this stage will be worthwhile.

Unspecified nouns
Example: People are good learners.

Challenge: Who specifically is a good learner?

Unspecified verbs
Example: They encourage me to learn.

Challenge: How specifically do they encourage you to learn?

Universal quantifiers
Example: Anyone can do that.

Challenge: Absolutely *anyone* can do that?

Or

Can you think of a time when someone couldn't do that?

Modal operators of possibility and necessity
Example: It's impossible to have learnt that material by that date.

Challenge: What's preventing you from learning it?

I have to do well on this course.

What would happen if you didn't?

Nominalization
Example: I didn't get any respect for that exercise.

Challenge: How would you like to be respected for that exercise?

Cause and effect
Example: When you look at me, I want to work harder.

Challenge: How does me looking at you make you want to work harder?

Another key aspect of gathering information is being alert enough to pick up on all the non-verbal cues which are given. This does not mean that the trainer should always automatically knee-jerk a response and immediately respond to a single yawn, but it does mean that the trainer should be sufficiently aware of everything that is going on.

Some trainers use what is known as the 'training state' to prepare themselves. This technique was covered in 2.1 Maintaining a positive personal state (page 33). This means:

- Getting to the training room (or as it should more appropriately be called, the learning room) before any of the learners arrive.
- Finding a central point from where you will do most of the training.
- Finding a spot above where the learner opposite you will be.
- Focusing with absolute attention on that spot.
- Gradually, *while still focusing on that spot*, taking in everything that you can see and are aware of, down the sides of the room, back to level with yourself, then behind you as well.

The key element in this exercise is in doing this while staying focused on the original spot. The purpose of the exercise is to create peripheral vision, so that you are aware of *everything* taking place in the room.

It is a very self-empowering skill for a trainer to have, and it also causes maximum impact and benefit for the learning group. Three hundred and sixty degree vision and sensitivity is a wonderful skill in the effective trainer's armoury.

GATHERING INFORMATION: EXERCISES

1. Listen for examples of violations and challenge (or just listen if that is appropriate).
2. With two colleagues: each person develops a list of violations in a particular category, puts them into a discussion. One other person has to spot the violations, the other person observes and gives feedback. Then swap roles, then swap roles again.

GATHERING INFORMATION: KEY POINTS

☐ Remember that internal experience interacts with external or sensory experience.
☐ Gather information regarding:
  – unspecified nouns;
  – unspecified verbs;
  – universal quantifiers;
  – modal operators of possibility and necessity;
  – nominalizations;
  – cause and effect.
☐ Use non-verbal communication to gather information.
☐ Use the trainer state to create total vision.

3.10 COMMUNICATING CLEARLY AND EFFECTIVELY

This is not just about the clear articulation of words and having well-produced handouts – important as these are. Communication is a total and constant process and everything trainers do or say, either verbally or non-verbally during the training will impact on their effectiveness.

This means using the appropriate visual, auditory and kinesthetic language, using non-verbal communication and the full range of techniques covered in this book. Particular insight into Meta Programs (see 4.21 Using Meta Programs, page 167) is very useful in this area as they help explain why people do what they do. One of the most commonly repeated quotes in NLP is that people do things for their reasons, *not* your reasons. This applies equally to learners. It is no use judging their response in this area by comparing it to the standards the trainer has. To quote another NLP maxim, 'The meaning of your communication is the response you get'.

Part of communicating clearly and effectively is to use positive language. This does not mean over hyping or 'flanelling' but focusing on what is working, picking up on strengths, when dealing with problems and weaknesses, picking up on what can be made to work in the situation. Equally this aspect of positive language applies to asking proper questions, giving feedback etc.

COMMUNICATING EFFECTIVELY: EXERCISE

As all NLP is about communicating effectively, any of the exercises in this book can be tried.

COMMUNICATING EFFECTIVELY: KEY ACTIONS

☐ Get all words, handouts, etc to a high standard.
☐ Remember that communication is a total process.
☐ Use non-verbal communication.
☐ Use all the techniques covered in this book.
☐ Use Meta Programs.
☐ Remember learners do things for their reasons, *not* your reasons.
☐ Remember the meaning of your communication is the response you get.
☐ Use positive language.

3.11 USING PRE-SUPPOSITIONS

Pre-suppositions are a very useful part of the trainer's skill base. As we have seen throughout this chapter, based on language, using the right words, in the right way, at the right time, makes a substantial shift in the learning taking place.

NLP itself is based on a number of pre-suppositions which we covered in the introductory section dealing with its origins; these are called operating principles.

Pre-suppositions that can be used by the trainer include:

● *When* you have learnt this subject...
● *When* you apply these skills back at work...
● *When* we come on to that topic...

Normally a 'when' properly framed will create a pre-supposition of further positive action. Used appropriately, therefore, they can be used to empower the learners for what is to come, whether it is inside the training or not. Most uses of language will contain some form of pre-supposition which will be apparent with careful listening.

USING PRE-SUPPOSITIONS: EXERCISES

1. Use a 'when' with learners at the beginning of a session to pre-suppose a later event.
2. Do 1 and use an embedded command as well.
3. Use differing emphasis, voice tones, representation systems, when using pre-suppositions.
4. For self, combine with visualizing and mental rehearsal to maintain a positive personal state.
5. Combine using pre-suppositions with any of the other relevant exercises in this book, eg outcomes.

USING PRE-SUPPOSITIONS: KEY POINTS

☐ Use a 'when' to establish future action.
☐ Use pre-suppositions to empower learners.
☐ Most uses of language contain a range of pre-suppositions.

3.12 USING EFFECTIVE QUESTIONS

Most of this chapter on getting the message across has featured using appropriate language techniques, and questions are a key part of this. The Meta Model, gathering information, sleight of mouth, even using embedded commands, all rely on effective use of questions.

In addition to these, using a simple dos and don'ts list will help ensure that the right questions are asked, but, more particularly, in the right way.

Combined with calibration with the person being asked the question, supported by creating rapport, language patterns and other NLP techniques, they form a useful part of the trainer's armoury.

Do	*Don't*
Ask one question at a time.	Ask multiple questions.
Ask questions.	Make statements.
Ask open questions.	Ask forced choice questions.
Ask probing open questions.	Ask closed questions.
Stay open and neutral.	Ask leading questions.
Clarify.	Jump to conclusions.
Ask short, to-the-point questions.	Ask long, complicated questions.
Be aware of non-verbals.	Use more non-verbals.
Be prepared to listen.	Switch off before they get to the real point.

USING EFFECTIVE QUESTIONS: EXERCISES

1. Practise using specific types of questions.
2. Practise deliberately avoiding using specific types of questions.
3.. Listen to the quality of questions other people use and the response they create.
4. Combine with any of the other relevant exercises in this book, eg creating rapport.
5. Watch and listen for verbal and non-verbal responses to certain questions.

USING EFFECTIVE QUESTIONS: KEY POINTS

☐ All of getting the message across is about the effective use of language; questions are a part of this.
☐ Quality questions produce quality results.

3.13 USING EYE ACCESSING CUES

For those people who only know one thing about NLP, it is probably eye accessing cues. Many people are aware that, when they watch someone thinking, the thinker's eyes move in various directions. These eye movements are indicative of how the person is processing the information inside their head and can reveal their preferences regarding how they prefer to be communicated with.

One of the helpful aspects of this is that it ties in with representation systems, language patterns and predicates, ie if a learner's eyes go up when they are thinking that would indicate a preference, at that moment, for processing in a visual way. This would be supported by the use of visual type words, eg focused, clear, picture, when responding.

The standard model of eye accessing cues is given in Figure 3.1.

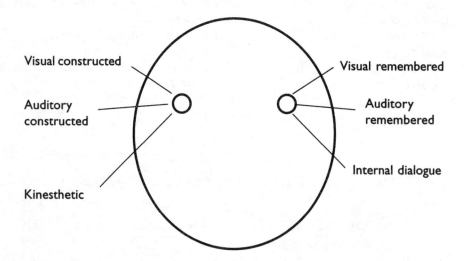

Note: This is when looking at the other person. It is also important to remember that a certain number of people, mainly left-handed people, will do this the other way round.

Figure 3.1 *Eye accessing cues*

Calibrating to eye accessing cues allows the trainer the opportunity to create rapport, pace and lead and get the message across in the most effective way for the learner.

In addition it allows trainers to find out their own preferences.

EYE ACCESSING CUES: EXERCISES

1. Ask questions to practise eye accessing cues, eg 'What colour was your first car?' 'What would your name sound like said backwards?' 'How did you feel when you passed your driving test?'
2. Calibrate to the eye accessing cues and listen to the language patterns and predicates used in response, check the match.
3. Watch for eye accessing cues in day-to-day conversations. Notice why there is rapport, what causes it. Do the same when rapport isn't achieved.
4. Watch for eye accessing cues with people on TV or in films.
5. Practise matching eye accessing cues with your responses using predicates and appropriate language.

EYE ACCESSING CUES: KEY POINTS

☐ Evidence of how learners are processing and thinking.
☐ Will match with language used.
☐ Allows trainer to create rapport, pace and lead.
☐ Helps the trainer recognize their own preferences.

BEING FLEXIBLE TO MEET THE NEEDS

4

BEING FLEXIBLE TO MEET THE NEEDS

'There are no difficult learners, only inflexible trainers.'
Anon

The whole art of achieving the desired outcomes for both the learners and the trainer is based upon flexibility.

One of the maxims of NLP is that if what you are doing doesn't work, *do something else*. Many trainers fall into the trap of doing more of what is already not working, rather than changing it. This does not, of course, mean becoming a loose cannon over-reacting to everything that occurs, but does mean knowing the outcomes clearly and being willing and able to respond in order to achieve them. None of the techniques covered in this chapter are necessarily better or worse than each other; they, along with the others covered in this book, need to be part of the trainer's repertoire.

4.1 GETTING PARTICIPANTS TO SET OWN GOALS

A fairly standard way to start most training events is to establish, not only the organizational goals that the trainer has been hired to deliver, but also the expectations and goals of the participants. Often this consists of a couple of pieces of flipchart hanging loosely from a wall which may or may not be referred to throughout the rest of the training.

The interesting point is that the evidence of Locke and Laham (1990), who surveyed over 400 studies on goals, leads overwhelmingly to the conclusion that difficult goals lead to better performance than easy, vague ones. The survey was based on 'results based on studies conducted in the US and seven other countries, on more than 40,000 subjects, 88 different tasks, time spans ranging from one minute to three years, and many different performance criteria, including behaviour change, quantity and quality outcomes and costs'.

In following up this work Ford (1992) decided that goal setting requires:

1. ample feedback to make corrections;
2. capability beliefs to sustain pursuit in the face of negative feedback;
3. actual skills to complete the task;
4. environment conducive to success.

The classic, and best-known, goal-setting model which is highly appropriate for training purposes is:

S   Specific
M   Measurable
A   Attainable
R   Realistic
T   Timebound

In addition it is useful where change is involved to clarify that the trainee:

●   wants to change;
●   knows what to change;
●   can respond to how to change;
●   has the opportunity to change.

The use of goal review sheets and/or action plans throughout the training are very useful to embed and review progress. In addition, where appropriate, small discussion or coaching groups can further assist this process if done on a regular basis. Also tasking individuals and groups is an effective strategy (see 4.22 Tasking people, page 184).

NLP itself uses an outcomes model. This is based on the same outcomes process that we covered in 2.5 Setting own personal outcomes (page 44), and is based on the standard NLP model:

Positive	Goal expressed in *positive* terms (not, what isn't wanted)?
Own part	Can actually be controlled by learner?
Specific	Outcome tangible and measurable?
Evidence	What is evidence in VAKOG language?
Ecology	Is it OK to do, balanced with other people, life, etc?
Action	Start doing it now.

Many learners who think that they are good at conventional goal setting find this process a lot harder than it looks. They are not used to some aspect or another. A recent example was someone who didn't want to be fat and did not (and felt they could not) specify the actual weight they wanted to attain. It took a little time for them to realize that this was the reason they hadn't achieved their outcome in the first place.

GETTING PARTICIPANTS TO SET OWN GOALS: EXERCISES

1. Use the NLP outcomes model, on issues connected with, and outside, the training area.
2. Use the SMART model, where appropriate.
3. Get participants to regularly review outcomes to establish good habits.

GETTING PARTICIPANTS TO SET OWN GOALS: KEY POINTS

☐ Get trainees to set goals per session and/or day.
☐ Ensure that the goals are demanding.
☐ Ensure that goals follow the SMART model.
☐ Use the NLP outcomes approach.
☐ Ensure that change goals answer the want to, what to, how to, opportunity to, questions.
☐ Use discussion groups to review progress.
☐ Use coaching groups to assist feedback.
☐ Use tasks with individuals and groups.
☐ Review progress regularly.

GETTING PARTICIPANTS TO SET OWN GOALS: CASE STUDY

In working on an ongoing self-development programme there was one participant who stated all her outcomes in negatives, ie describing what she didn't want. In reviewing what had happened in her life to date, she felt that she had failed at everything, but didn't know why. Through creating rapport, calibration, using language patterns, she was able to develop a positive goal which met the NLP criteria.

Because she felt that she was a failure at work, she decided to choose an out of work goal first of all, to learn a language to conversational standard, within six months. The outcome was constantly reviewed throughout the programme and achieved to the extent of taking a holiday in France and not having to use English.

Encouraged by this success, she developed outcomes for her job and is currently enjoying her work, and being appreciated for it.

Outcomes don't have to be set for such a long period, they can be established for a presentation, meeting or interview. Reviewed they can, like many other NLP techniques, become generative, ie become more effective through repeated use.

4.2 PACING AND LEADING A GROUP

Pacing and leading are built on creating effective rapport (see 1.2 Creating rapport, page 15). In rapport we went through the basic steps for being aware of a learner's or a group's non-verbal communication and matching or cross-over matching it to create rapport.

Once having achieved rapport, it is then possible to pace and lead the learner and/or group by the trainer using their own non-verbal communication. This will result in significant changes in physiology, verbal responses and attitude and response from the learner and/or group.

Taking this process one stage at a time, pacing means meeting the other person(s) where they are, matching some part of their ongoing experience. There are a number of ways that pacing can be achieved: non-verbal communication, speech patterns (this includes rate of speech, tonality, volume, words, phrases), breathing and eye accessing cues.

In deciding what to pace it is important to look and listen for what seems to be the most important to the learner/group. A specific process for pacing is:

- Look for breathing and body movements.
- Listen to the language patterns.
- Pace breathing.
- Pace body movements.
- Pace language patterns.

Note: It is important that this part of the process is carried out with respect. Crossing arms immediately after a learner has done so may not be respectful and may, therefore, cause a negative response. People who are adept at this technique refer to 'a dance over a period of time'.

- Discuss areas of common interest (try chunking up and down – see 4.24 Using chunking, page 185).
- Reflect back words and phrases, or in responding use similar word patterns, ie visual, quality, kinesthetic, metaphors.
- Look for volume of speech, voice tonality, eye blink rates, eye accessing cues.
- Pace whichever of these seem to be the most important.

The technique of cross-over matching is required when the learner and/or group use examples that the trainer does not want to pace, eg irregular, stressful breathing, inappropriate language. Pacing by using a different response, eg tapping a foot in response to threatening head gestures, can be just as effective as the more overt pacing discussed above. Cross-over pacing can also be important when more conventional forms of pacing could be perceived as threatening or mocking.

Although pacing is a very straightforward technique, trainers who have not come across it described this way before sometimes worry about 'being spotted' trying to create rapport and pacing. Normally the people being dealt with are so into their own agenda they don't realize and even if they do, they take it as a compliment that you are sufficiently interested in them to make the effort. Remember that pacing will only work when it is done with respect, doing it to manipulate will be noted at an unconscious level by the learner/group and will damage the relationship.

It is also important to remember that some form of pacing is the basis for most kinds of human communication. The conversation with a friend regarding the family, hobbies, car, sporting interests, holds examples of pacing before getting to a specific point of that particular communication.

Following on from pacing is leading. This is where, having achieved rapport through pacing, the trainer leads the learner/group into a new direction, or at a quicker pace than they would have moved normally. Leading will not work unless proper and considerate matching and pacing have already taken place. Therefore the simple method to follow is: match, pace, pace, pace, lead. This may need to be done on a number of occasions in any one communication and therefore requires constant attention to the other person.

I once heard described the work of Janet Adler with autistic children, which is an interesting example of the use of pacing and leading. Initially, she paced their non-verbal communication by paying very close attention to their behaviour and, where appropriate, entering their world. When they clapped, she clapped; when they moved their heads in a certain way, so did she; when they assumed a particular body position, so did she.

This pacing went on for a very long time before she then began to lead them through some of the normal stages of development. After a period of time the autistic children were able to respond by making eye contact, accepting touch and affection, and, eventually, by speaking.

This example is a good illustration of pacing and leading. The leading stage involves building on the rapport created by pacing and then creating a direction using exactly the same range of responses that produced the rapport in the first place, ie breathing, posture, body movement, gestures, language patterns, voice volume and tonality, blink rates, eye accessing cues.

PACING AND LEADING A GROUP: CASE STUDIES

Two specific examples of pacing and leading are outlined below:

1. A training environment where a nervous learner was fidgeting and using broken sentences in a low, hesitant voice whenever the trainer spoke to him. The trainer recognized what was taking place and matched the learner by body posture, movement and slowing down her voice speed. She also cross-over matched by using slight hand gestures to match the breaks in the voice of the learner. Having received non-verbal feedback that rapport had been achieved (by noting breathing and skin colour changes) the trainer then raised the volume of her voice to a more normal conversational level and spoke slightly more quickly to fill the hesitant gaps. By the end of the session the learner was talking normally to the trainer and was also observed in animated conversation over the lunch break.

2. During a training course on a new performance management process a middle-aged, senior manager became irate about being 'forced' to attend a training course about a process that he had no particular faith in. This struck a chord with other course members who egged him on as he became more and more vociferous, and his voice became louder and his gestures and language more threatening.

    The trainer stayed calm and focused and, rather than defend himself, or the course, raised the volume of his voice to, *but not above*, the speaker's, while at the same time matching his language patterns, which were predominantly visual and metaphors, eg 'I can't see the point in this', 'The trouble is here no one has a vision about what's right', etc. At the same time the trainer started to use 'I' language instead of 'We', thus adopting a basic assertive stance.

    After a number of exchanges of dialogue, the trainer lowered his voice volume to a normal conversational level, started using visual language with a more positive intent and started to use 'We' phrases again, eg 'It's vital that we can all see where this leads us' and 'The benefits of this process will be visible to all once we've implemented it'.

    Within a few minutes normal conversation was resumed and the course proceeded as if nothing had happened.

It is possible to practise developing these skills and these exercises can be used by trainers among themselves or with friends, or in a learning environment to help learners develop the skills.

PACING AND LEADING A GROUP: EXERCISES

These exercises are designed for three people A, B and C, but can be done with two or four with slight modifications.

These exercises are taken from *Mega-Teaching and Learning* (1985), by C Van Nagel, Edward Reese, Maryann Reese and Robert Siudzinski, but other versions are readily available from a variety of sources and trainers can also create their own.

Exercise 1: *Mirroring*

Purpose: To improve skills in observing and mirroring.
To improve skills in matching body changes.

Directions: A and B face each other. A mirrors and matches B. C stands behind B, facing and observing A. B is directed to talk about two specific experiences that resulted in different emotional responses, such as a successful lesson, winning a sports event or achieving an award. For example, while B is describing number 1 and displaying excitement, A mirrors the behaviour and expressions of B. While B is describing experience number 2 and displaying embarrassment, A again mirrors the behaviour and expressions of B. B then selects one of the experiences and re-creates it. While B is again describing it, *internally* to themselves this time, A mirrors the behaviour and expressions of B. C must then determine from watching A, while *not hearing* B, which experience B is expressing.

Exercise 2: *Matching and mismatching*

Purpose: To increase perceptual skills.
To develop flexibility in mismatching skills.

Directions: B is asked to leave the room. Prior to B's return A is instructed to talk, but mismatch B. C is instructed to match B's breathing. Upon returning to the room, A and B begin a conversation for an allotted time (3–5 minutes). At the end of this time A and B share observations of what they have experienced.

Note: Observe that when rapport with B has been gained through matched breathing (by C), B frequently begins to direct most conversation to C rather than A.

Exercise 3: *Building rapport – pacing and leading*

Purpose: To further build and improve skills in building rapport, pacing and leading.

Directions: Rapport is established by A, who is conversing with B. For a short period A breaks rapport with B by mismatching. A then re-establishes rapport with B. Observations are described by C.

Exercise 4: *Building rapport, pacing and leading*
Purpose: To improve skills in building rapport and pacing.
Directions: A and B begin discussing a disappointing experience. A should pace B with breathing, body movements, facial expressions, eye movements, eye blinks, voice tempo, posture, idiosyncratic movements, etc. A should use at least one cross-over mirroring technique. A must change one of the above rapport building behaviours after rapport has been established. If B follows A's lead, increased rapport is established. C observes and reports feedback in sensory-specific language. For example, 'You paced B's breathing with your hand and cross-over matched B's head nods by moving your foot'.

Exercise 5: *Any of the relevant exercises from 1.2 Creating rapport (page 15)*
These exercises will not only develop skills and improve powers of observation and perception, they will also be great fun to do and provide a good foundation for further skill development.

PACING AND LEADING A GROUP: KEY POINTS

☐ Create rapport as a first step.
☐ Look (and listen and feel) for:
  – breathing and body movement ;
  – language patterns;
  – breathing.
☐ Remember that it is 'a dance over a period of time'.
☐ Do everything with respect for the other people and within a purposeful intention.
☐ Use cross-over matching where appropriate.
☐ Use leading by following the process of:
  – match;
  – pace;
  – pace;
  – pace;
  – lead.
☐ Try using pacing and leading in live situations inside and outside training events.
☐ Practise using the exercises with colleagues.

4.3 USING NON-VERBAL COMMUNICATION

A great deal has been written regarding non-verbal communication, or body language as it is sometimes called. Most of the popular views are derived from the work of Albert Mehrabian, who stated that the emotional impact of communication could be broken down into:

55% body language
38% voice – tone, pitch, pace, etc
7% actual words used.

This research has often been misconstrued and taken absolutely literally. The key point that Mehrabian was making was, that if there was a lack of sincerity or conviction in the words or how they were said or a mixed signal with the body language, people normally, consciously or unconsciously, form their own view of the truth from the 93 per cent outside the specific words used.

One other point that is also worthy of comment, is the use of the phrase 'body language'. Although having the benefit of being readily understood by a majority of people, it barely does justice to the complexity and subtlety of its subject. A lot of people only look for the overt crossing of the arms or legs, rather than the more revealing blink rates, skin colour changes, breathing patterns, minute body movement changes, etc.

This, coupled with the tendency to generalize and attach meaning to these overt patterns, eg when people cross their arms they are being defensive, means that much very useful information can be missed, or at best misconstrued.

The implications for the trainer who has an awareness of, and can use, non-verbal communication are vast. Although initially it can seem daunting to have to fine-tune to large numbers of people in a training programme the benefits are enormous.

There are two aspects for a trainer in using non-verbal communication effectively:

● being aware of others';
● being aware of one's own.

Being aware of other people's non-verbal communication
Earlier in this book we discussed creating rapport and using perceptual positions. Both of these techniques incorporate an awareness of other people's non-verbal communication. Indeed, it could be argued that any trainer who does not have this awareness will find it extremely difficult to run learner-effective training programmes. Because, unless they are able to pick up the signals and respond appropriately, the training will not achieve all of its outcomes.

This does not mean that the trainer must become a 'puppet on a string' who, on observing a non-verbal communication shift, changes content and style immediately in order to keep the training on track. Rather it means that the trainer is (a) sufficiently aware and in tune with the learners; and (b) able to respond flexibly and appropriately, which could mean just carrying on in order to make the learning as effective as possible. Specific non-verbal techniques that work are:

- Match breathing and gestures.
- Match physical height in conversation, ie don't stand over a learner when coaching them, match by sitting or crouching next to them.
- Use lots of nods and non-verbals when a learner is responding rather than jumping in to show you understand.
- Create learner to learner non-verbal communication by use of energy bursts.
- Use language to create non-verbal communication – 'you can all sit back now and enjoy this video prior to us putting it into action afterwards'.
- Run a session on actively listening – non-verbally.
- Act as a sounding board, ie *visibly* listen without offering your own solutions – this then allows for an equal response when you do speak.
- Recognize non-verbally when a questioner has received an answer they can accept or work on, or alternatively when they haven't.
- If the going gets hard create an immediate energy break.

Being aware of and using your own non-verbal communication

As well as being aware of, and fine-tuning to, the learners' non-verbal communication, it is vital that a trainer is equally aware of his own. Our physiology is connected with our emotional state and thinking and this can be particularly obvious to a group of trainees. Therefore, the potential for trainers using words that pretend that they are comfortable when the non-verbal communication indicates something completely different, is very high. This is not to say that becoming an automaton who is so self-controlled that you reveal nothing is recommended. Rather it is a case of being open with your feelings and what is happening. Therefore, 'having nerves' is fine. The question is how to make them work for you. Virtually every type of performer accepts that butterflies are normal and responds to them as part of a positive process.

Eric Jensen in his book *Super-teaching* (1994a), quotes a number of non-verbal techniques to help:

- Systematically scan the room to create and maintain learner awareness.
- Look for small, less overt signals, eg shifting posture, breathing, raised eye brows, smiles, a look between two people, and pause briefly with an enquiring look to see if the question or comment emerges.

- When someone does speak step back rather than forward to include all the other learners in the process.
- Make eye contact and, if appropriate, smile with your eyes.
- Should an interaction occur shift your non-verbal communication to a sharing, open posture rather than stiffen and become the formal presenter.
- Maintain an interested look when both you and they are speaking.
- Maintain a full-front stance or alternatively a V formation.
- If you need to use your hands use open gestures rather than pointing, as this can cause alienation.
- If one learner is tending to dominate break eye contact, politely, and scan the rest of the group.

A specific exercise developed by Robert Dilts (1994) is as follows.

1. Pick a topic that is important or challenging to present.
2. Pick a series of non-verbal messages that you wish to get across, eg:
   - your own state and views;
   - type of relationship with the audience;
   - desired state for learners to be in;
   - level of focus of the communication.
3. Decide how you could use voice tone, gestures, spatial location to communicate the non-verbal messages.
4. Do the input/session 'live'.
5. After the input/session each learner records the non-verbal message received and the signals which were picked up on.
6. Group and trainer compare 'intended' and 'received' non-verbal messages.

This is a very powerful and open way of developing skills and receiving feedback. It can be done more informally by asking for feedback at the end of a session, over a cup of coffee at a break, or completely outside the training room. It has also been used as a full-blown training activity when the outcome has been to develop non-verbal sensory skills. It can also form the basis for using reverse tests (see 4.14, page 148). Used this way, all participants, learners and trainers develop important skills with mutual benefit.

USING NON-VERBAL COMMUNICATION: EXERCISES

1. The exercise covered in this section.
2. Watch people on TV or films, in documentaries, chat shows, turn the volume down, observe and reflect on the dance of body language.
3. From a distance, watch strangers meet, observe and reflect on the dance of body language.
4. From a distance, watch people who are friends meet, observe and reflect on the dance of body language.
5. Develop an awareness of your own (and others') non-verbal communication in a variety of situations, eg at a meeting, over lunch, giving a presentation, on the phone.

USING NON-VERBAL COMMUNICATION: KEY POINTS

☐ Remember the 55% body language, 38% voice (tone, pitch, pace, tonality etc), 7% words rule.
☐ Go beyond body language into non-verbal communication.
☐ Be aware of others' non-verbal communication:
   – match breathing and gestures;
   – match physical height in conversation;
   – use energy bursts;
   – use language to create non-verbal communication;
   – run a session on non-verbal active listening;
   – demonstrate high quality active listening as a role-model.
☐ Beware of your own non-verbal communication:
   – match your physiology with language used;
   – maintain learner awareness;
   – fine-tune to subtle signals;
   – step back when someone asks a question if there is a danger of excluding the group;
   – smile with your eyes;
   – use an open posture;
   – maintain an interested look;
   – maintain a full-frontal or V stance;
   – use open gestures, rather than point;
   – scan the whole group;
   – use the exercises to practise and get feedback.

USING NON-VERBAL COMMUNICATION: CASE STUDY

A group of production mangers was attending a course on selection interviewing. One of them, who admitted he was nervous, was very erratic in his gestures and non-verbal communication. During his first 'live' interview this made the candidate nervous, and the candidate gave this as feedback in the review session.

Before the second interview, outside the formal training, he worked through two of the exercises from maintaining a positive personal state, and agreed to the outcome of, if required, trying a pace and lead.

At the start of his next interview the candidate was jerky in his movements. The interviewer cross-over mirrored him by tapping with his pencil. Having achieved rapport he then slowed the tempo of his tapping, finally putting the pencil down. By this time the candidate was sitting in a relaxed, open posture conducting a normal conversation.

4.4 CREATING GROUP DYNAMICS

Every trainer has a wide variety of ways of creating group dynamics, from the use of syndicate exercises, particularly after a break, to use of their own favourite materials and specific interpersonal skills.

A number of techniques already covered in this book work very powerfully in creating group dynamics. (See 1.4 Creating rituals and engaging emotions (page 25), 4.1 Getting participants to set own goals (page 105), 1.5 Using exercise bursts to create energy (page 27), 2.8 Using a variety of training techniques (page 51), 2.6 Using anchors (page 45).) There are additional ways of achieving this objective.

The first point is that most cues are taken from trainers themselves. This means that a consistency of approach and energy, a willingness to listen and open out, the ability to respond flexibly to a variety of situations with purpose and commitment, will produce consistently high group dynamics.

Many of the most effective trainers use training by the 'Tai Kwan Do' technique rather than the training by 'Mike Tyson' technique. All this means is that the more important it is for a group to have high dynamics, the more important it is for the trainer to do less overtly and to recognize the fulcrum of the group focus and energy and create direction from that source. Always, of course, bearing in mind the specific outcomes for that particular training.

Put another way it means if in doubt, do less, but do it more effectively. Another metaphor would be the surfer whose skill lies in using the energy of the wave to get to the beach. The skill is in the timing, the balance and the judgement.

This is even more important should there be a particular difficulty on the course, eg a really awkward person or a total loss of group energy. It may be appropriate in these circumstances for the trainer to 'do more' in order to regain control or the initiative. Equally it may be more effective to use third position (see 2.7 Using perceptual positions, page 48) to find the energy of the situation and use it to move forward, rather than become emotionally embroiled and throw energy and good intentions at the situation.

One key skill in creating group dynamics is staying fully-tuned to the group, rather than becoming preoccupied with your own performance. This is actually harder than it sounds but is a prerequisite for the effective trainer. This involves a number of skills covered in other parts of this book, in particular, body movements, breathing, gestures, voice volume and tonality, facial expressions, mannerisms (including some very subtle ones, eg rubbing hands, playing with ears).

A lot of this information is passed on by individuals and groups without them realizing it, but it will be very visible to the perceptive trainer.

Based upon the work of Eric Jenson – who is an essential read on these skills – keeping learners involved can be as straightforward as:

- Create agreed signals from the group to you to give instant feedback, eg literally the thumbs up.
- If having to give an input, do it in small chunks and then ask questions about it.
- Use embedded commands.
- Rather than ask the whole group if they have questions, ask a particular location, eg 'who on this side has any questions?'
- Use flipcharts posted round the wall – if anyone doesn't understand something or wants more information, they go to a particular flipchart and put their name on it, or tick a flipchart with the topic on it. If there are more than x per cent of the group ticked, the trainer responds accordingly.
- Use unfinished sentences – let them finish them.
- Ensure that all equipment is being used to its maximum advantage. This includes blackboards, flipcharts, OHPs, videos.
- Use posters, etc effectively. A lot of time will be spent in the training environment and that can become a negative anchor; therefore, make it lively, bright and positive, use quotes for day, comments from the previous sessions or day's training, flag up topics still to come.
- Use colours appropriately rather than just using the flipchart pens provided by the venue. Research suggests that the following colours create certain associations:
  - **black:** dominant, dying, serious, intrusive, cold – limit use as much as possible;
  - **orange:** active, playful, communicative, assertive – could be used more often;

- **red:** urgent, present-time oriented, feelings, heart, important – limited usage keeps impact high;
- **green:** soothing, future-oriented, relaxing, growth, positive – has widespread uses;
- **blue:** strong, past-oriented, tradition, factual, cold, impersonal – use when presenting controversial information.

- Train learners in specific note taking techniques. Everyone sitting horizontal, gazing at the front of the room will not create high dynamics. Getting learners to use techniques such as mind mapping, using coloured pens laid on by the trainer, can help. In addition, at the end of a session if only a small number have used a particular technique, eg mind mapping, get someone to review the session using their mind map. Used appropriately this will assist the learning, develop the individual and encourage others to use the technique (or find one of their own).

- Use music to create extra dynamics, eg themes to well-known films. Eric Jenson (1994b) quotes research carried out by Manfred Clives of Australia, Georgi Lazanov of Bulgaria, Don Campbell of Texas, Steven Halpern of California and Don Schuster of Iowa which measured the effects of music on the nervous system. The evidence shows that the emotions, heart rate, posture, respiratory system and mental images of the learner are all affected by music. This means that mood and a state change can take place and, therefore, direct access to behavioural change can be gained.

- Use a wide variety of language so that there is something for all types, ie visual, auditory and kinesthetic. Where appropriate be dramatic, if the point is an important one don't be afraid to say so and show the group you care about the point, and them and their response to it.

- Always ensure that all materials, eg slides, videos are right up to date. The effect of an old-fashioned hair style or shirt collar on a video, can lose a lot of good learning points, even with an older audience.

- Always ensure that the information offered is totally up to date. Quote the most recent information. Where this is a few years old, put it into a current context. Use current business organizational or educational language. Mention instances from current situations in the media.

- Don't over communicate, keep sentences brief and to the point.

- Use positive words and phrases, particularly on key points, eg don't say 'You may find this topic a bit difficult', because, guess what – they will. Go for what is purposeful and positive.

- Provide positive associations between topics in order to reinforce previous learning, eg 'this is another aspect of... which we covered yesterday'. You can get them to explain what the association is.

- Use quotes and anecdotes. There are dangers in being perceived as an anecdotal trainer, but used effectively they can be very successful. Ensuring that they relate directly to the topic, people will remember them for years to come. Every trainer has their own repertoire of quotes and anecdotes, but again they should be used constructively.
- Use humour.
- Use constant affirmation of group progress and always be clear regarding how far the group is through a topic.
- Use success stories of either well-known people and/or previous learners of the particular topic.

CREATING GROUP DYNAMICS: EXERCISES

1. Use some of the skills covered in this book, eg using third position, using smaller chunks, exercise bursts, evaluate success by observation and feedback.
2. Be prepared to try any of the list should training become bogged down.

CREATING GROUP DYNAMICS: KEY POINTS

- ☐ Use rituals, setting own goals, exercise bursts and anchors.
- ☐ Be consistently open and energetic.
- ☐ Use 'Tai Kwan Do' rather than 'Mike Tyson' strategies.
- ☐ Use the third perceptual position.
- ☐ Stay tuned to the group.
- ☐ Be aware of all the non-verbal communication.
- ☐ Use signals, small chunks, embedded commands, ask questions, use flipcharts, unfinished sentences, proper equipment, posters, appropriate colours, note taking, music, language, drama, effective materials and information, current examples, the name game, short sentences, positive words and phrases, positive association, quotes and anecdotes, humour, constant affirmation and success stories.

4.5 CHANGING LEARNER STATES

Every trainer has a range of war stories regarding the most difficult individual or groups they have ever encountered, and how they overcame the problem. It can be easy to fall into blame, or be diverted by the one individual who appears to be negative and be side-tracked or lose the group at large.

It is important to remember that no matter how negative the individual or group is, there is something that they are positive about. In other words there is a key to everyone. Also it's hardly a surprise if people are negative if they have been 'sent' to somewhere they don't want to be, to do something they don't want to do, with someone they don't want to be with. One way to get over this problem early on is to introduce the topic using the 4 MAT approach covered in 4.10 Creating new learning patterns, page 132.

Other techniques covered in this book that can also be used include:

- creating rapport;
- pacing and leading a group;
- getting participants to set own goals (again and again);
- using language patterns;
- answering the four key questions:
  - Why? Why are we here?
  - What? What are we going to do/cover?
  - How? How are we going to do it?
  - What if? Related to back at work applications.

The list above covers everything in this book, and this is the real issue. Effective trainers need to have all of these at their disposal, be flexible and willing enough to try them and willing to try something else if one thing doesn't work. The situation to avoid is becoming equally stuck in a particular state – this may just wedge both parties in even tighter.

As the quote at the beginning of this chapter says: 'There are no difficult learners, only inflexible trainers.'

CHANGING LEARNER STATES: EXERCISES

1. Use any of the relevant exercises covered in other sections, eg creating rapport, pacing and leading a group, getting participants to set own goals, using language patterns, etc.
2. Practise use of specific skills in a variety of situations to also develop flexibility.
3. Use third position on self to self-coach and help evaluate and give feedback later.

CHANGING LEARNER STATES: KEY POINTS

- ☐ Stay positive and focused.
- ☐ Use the
  - Why – we are here;
  - What – we are going to do;
  - How – we are going to do it;
  - What if – future uses and applications.
- ☐ Use creating rapport/rituals and engaging emotions or any of the other techniques covered in this book.
- ☐ Be flexible.

CHANGING LEARNER STATES: CASE STUDY

In running a briefing session for a group of managers prior to the implementation of a new culture programme, it was apparent, by calibrating the majority of participants, that they were following a company procedure with which they didn't fully agree. As the purpose of the briefing was to equip them with the knowledge and skills to prepare their subordinates for the training programme, this presented an obvious issue.

The real issue to them was not what was being done, or how it was going to happen, but what would happen back at work, ie the what if – future uses and applications aspects.

Rather than force them through a long drawn out theoretical debate, the trainer concentrated on the 'what if', they agreed individual and departmental outcomes for both the training and the implementation and the briefing was considered useful and successful.

Later when the full training was carried out, participants arrived in a relaxed, open state of anticipation and contributed fully to the process.

4.6 USING HUMOUR

The effective use of humour is one of the most powerful tools in the trainer's repertoire. The ability to change direction, optimize a particular moment, defuse a tricky situation, settle a group or an individual down, add emphasis to a point, can make a tremendous difference to the learnings that emerge from a training session.

One of the difficulties regarding humour is actually capturing the essence or nuances of it in print. The difference between the humour of the North East and the Devonian is very significant, but equally effective, and these differences can still apply even with today's mass communications via television, radio and the other media.

Another aspect of this is that quite often the humorous comment doesn't look funny when it is written down. A lot can depend on the timing and the specific situation and it is normally these factors which make a particular comment humorous. The best forms of humour normally seem to have a strong degree of perception in them which means something to those involved even if they don't necessarily agree with it.

It is this latter skill that can be very useful to trainers who want to make their training sessions memorable, always remembering that the use of humour is intended to supplement good training, rather than be a substitute for it.

Humour is a much discussed topic but not one that is examined thoroughly and written up. One book that does this is *Taking Humour Seriously* by Jerry Palmer, who is Professor of Communications at London

Guildhall University. This book takes a classical look at humour from Freud to anthropology and from literary criticism to biology, and it is a worthwhile read for those seriously interested in the subject.

As part of an NLP master practitioner training attended in 1994, I carried out a modelling (see 2.4 Behaviour modelling and strategies, page 40) project on the uses of humour as a management skill. This was based on the interpersonal aspects, not telling jokes. Although the conclusions are in 'NLP speak' a summary of the key skills is outlined below for the use of the trainer (they are all topics covered in this book).

- Believe that humour can always be used and have an appropriateness, although the type of humour may vary dependent on the specific situation.
- Have the ability to use first, second and third positions to choose the right moment, style, etc.
- Use second position and rapport and physiology skills to 'read' the response.
- Use appropriate language to pace and lead people.
- Use humour to create anchors.
- See the possibility to use humour.
- Chunk up to hit a common thread.
- Use internal reference with external check.
- Be willing to use humour now for greater gain later.
- Do not take a limiting decision about your own ability to be funny.
- Use humour to create positive learnings.
- Use a variety of linguistic patterns, eg metaphor, sleight of mouth and, in particular, reframing.
- Be flexible and aware.
- Use match pace, pace, pace, lead or the opposite, ie deliberately interrupt a pattern in order to move things forward.
- Have an objective for the intervention.
- Use internal dialogue as a 'sounding board'.

Each of these skills could, of course, be broken down even further if necessary. In fact, each skill could be modelled in its own right. These results were based on 19 people who were perceived as being effective in using humour as an interpersonal skill.

Another useful article is 'The effective use of humour in human resource development' by Ozzie Dean, published in the *Developing Human Resources Annual* (1993). In this article Dean summarizes a number of studies of the uses of humour in a variety of situations. In all cases teachers who used humour or created and/or allowed an atmosphere of fun and play were rated more favourably by their students (Abramis, 1991). In addition where similar work was carried out with managers Abramis (1991), Duncan and Feisal (1989) and Kiechell (1983) reported an increase in creativity, productivity, motivation and satisfaction when enjoyment in the office was emphasized. A decrease in anxiety and depression was also noted.

Dean summarizes ten guidelines for effective use of humour, these are prefaced by two cautions:

Caution 1   Never introduce yourself in a humorous manner, unless your reputation has preceded you.

Caution 2   Never use humour to conceal a lack of preparation or inadequate knowledge of the subject matter.

Point 1   Make fun of yourself, not others.

Point 2   Laugh with people, not at them.

Point 3   Select material that relates to your topic or listeners.

Point 4   Believe in your material.

Point 5   Deliver your material well.

Point 6   Learn techniques for good delivery.

Point 7   Avoid ethnic put downs.

Point 8   Avoid sexist put downs.

Point 9   Give listeners permission to laugh.

Point 10   Use 'savers' if a story or joke doesn't work.

USING HUMOUR: EXERCISES

1. Use any of the skills covered in this section, eg first, second, third position, using language patterns, using humour to create anchors, matching and leading, etc. Exercises on all these skills are covered in this book under their titles.
2. Practise using skills outside as well as inside the training area.
3. Use the outcomes model to set goals based on humour.
4. Observe how other people use humour and the effect it has.
5. Model someone's strategy for using humour.

USING HUMOUR: KEY POINTS

☐ Effective humour is based on perception.
☐ Humour can be analysed for its strategies and modelled using NLP techniques.
☐ Effective humour produces increases in creativity, productivity, motivation and satisfaction.
☐ Equally, it causes a decrease in anxiety and depression.
☐ Use Ozzie Dean's ten rules.
　 – Make fun of self, not others.
　 – Laugh with people, not at them.

- Select material that relates to your topic or listeners.
- Believe in your material.
- Deliver your material well.
- Learn techniques for good delivery.
- Avoid ethnic put downs.
- Avoid sexist put downs.
- Give listeners permission to laugh.
- Use 'savers' if a story or joke doesn't work.

4.7 SWITCHING ROLES AND STYLES

One very useful skill for the effective trainer is the ability to switch roles and styles. This can be of particular use in creating and maintaining high expectations, creating energy and unsticking people (see separate headings in this book) but is also helpful in ensuring that the trainer does not become stereotyped or trapped into one particular style, even if that style has been successful in the past.

As was stated in the first section in Chapter 1, Styles of training, Wheeler and Marshall (1986) developed a model of trainer styles. These were listener, director, interpreter and coach. It is vital that the effective trainer can adapt the particular style required at a given time and then switch effortlessly into another one as appropriate.

As far as I am aware, no statistical evaluation has taken place regarding trainers' preference for one particular style and their ability to switch appropriately between them. However, if the pattern that emerges from some standard management models, eg Hersey and Blanchard's (1982) Situational Leadership applies, most trainers will over-use the one they feel comfortable with, or have had the most success with in the past, and also lack the flexibility to change style appropriately. A great deal of interesting work remains to be done in this area, and NLP could contribute a great deal in taking this work forward.

As part of the ability to switch styles appropriately, it is also vital to be able to switch roles. This means using the whole range of skills that are available, eg being able to move from giving information to being the questioner, the giver of feedback, the summarizer, the tester of understanding, all within a short period of time and with skill and poise. Equally it involves utilizing all of the skills covered in this book and having fun while doing so.

The picture that may emerge from all of this is a long way from some people's traditional notion of a trainer as a purveyor of knowledge (and maybe skills). As the fountainhead of all knowledge and wisdom casting pearls before swine. The whole of the management movement has gathered pace over the last few years and the effective trainer needs to be seen to be leading that advance rather than hanging on to its shirt tails for dear life. The old saying 'those that can do, those that can't teach' is quoted less and less nowadays, but we still have some way to go to be seen as leading the change.

SWITCHING ROLES AND STYLES: EXERCISES

1. Do exercises on any of the skills and techniques covered in this book which you believe would help you switch role and style more effectively, eg creating group dynamics, using language patterns, being a learning trainer, pacing and leading a group.
2. Observe to see if learners switch roles and styles as well, at what point and how do they do it, what effect does it have?
3. Watch other trainers, see how they do it, what works, what doesn't.

SWITCHING ROLES AND STYLES: KEY POINTS

☐ Move between listener, director, interpreter and coach styles.
☐ Move between all the roles required of the trainer, eg summarizer, questioner, etc.
☐ Be seen to be leading the process of management change.

SWITCHING ROLES AND STYLES: CASE STUDY

A training course on coaching skills was going particularly well. The participants were open, visibly enjoying the course and willing to take on board new ideas.

In the session just after lunch, the trainer, whose natural style was coach as well, realized that, although the training was proving to be enjoyable, she was in danger of not actually achieving the objectives of the day. Therefore, she decided that she needed to move briefly into a more director style but follow it up by more listening before coming back to the coaching style.

In doing this, she was aware that she could cause some confusion and break rapport, so she decided to match the group in terms of posture and language patterns before leading them into the new style. By calibrating to the group she knew that this had been achieved and then moved into the more director style, then into the listening, then back into the coaching.

At the end of the course, on the feedback forms, a number of the participants said that, although they had been enjoying the course, at one point, just after lunch, they were getting lost and unsure as to what its real purpose was. They felt that the trainer had recognized this and responded appropriately to help them achieve their objectives.

4.8 BEING AWARE OF INVISIBLES (VALUES, BELIEFS, IDENTITY)

This is a vital area for the trainer and one that can make the difference between success and failure. It can be very easy to blunder unawares into a situation and ruin the impact of what, up until then, has been a good session.

The logical levels model has been worked on by many people in NLP, in particular Robert Dilts (Figure 4.1). It is a very useful tool in these situations.

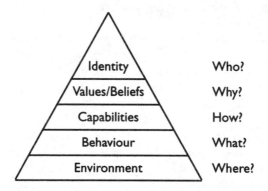

Figure 4.1 *Logical levels model – 1*

In using this model the levels of environment and behaviour are visible and some of the capabilities, but the other three layers are not. Another way to look at this is illustrated in Figure 4.2.

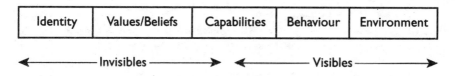

Figure 4.2 *Logical levels model – 2*

Dealt with in an open, constructive, purposeful way the visibles are undeniable, fact based and less emotive. Attacking (if that is how it is perceived) someone at the higher or invisible levels will almost certainly create a difficult situation.

Learners may have all sorts of issues regarding their capabilities, eg not being good with their hands, not being good with numbers, being better at something than other people, that they will bring to the session with them, but may or may not be open in sharing.

At a higher level learners are often not very explicit about their values and beliefs, but should the trainer offend these in any way serious harm can be done. Learners will often use very vague abstract and subjective sounding language when talking about issues related to values, beliefs and identity. This can sometimes confuse the unknowing trainer who does not realize the true level of depth and feeling that lie beneath the surface.

There are a number of techniques for eliciting values and helping (if it is appropriate) learners to recognize and utilize them for themselves. When people are being trained in NLP itself, a lot of the techniques and exercises are overtly aimed at the higher levels of the logical levels model. In more normal trainings the trainer needs to be equally aware, while not dealing with them as directly.

One exercise that can be very useful on all sorts of courses is called 'Hierarchy of Values'. Learners work in pairs A–B.

B asks A what is important to them about a particular topic, eg their job, or a specific part of it, or something outside work such as their family or their hobbies.

B allows and helps A to articulate as many words as emerge *without* judging or analysing them, just drawing them out and writing them down. B can then ask A which are the most important in priority order or, if this proves to be too difficult, start at the other end and B asks A which is the least important or which one could be let go of first.

Sometimes people will try and cluster various values together but with appropriate support and skills from B, A can finish up, in a very short time, with a useful list of their values in a particular context. It is worth emphasizing the point that the hierarchy of values established is specific to a particular context, eg work, family, hobbies, and that just doing it once for a few minutes does not mean that all the values for that individual have been identified.

However, this exercise used in specific ways, eg what is important about training, what is important about self-development or learning, can be very revealing to the individual and can cause maximum impact during a learning session.

Another well-known exercise is the NLP systemic belief approach:

- Decide on an outcome you want.
- Consider the following statements, marking from 1–10 your level of belief in each. (1 being lowest, 10 being highest):
  - My goal is desirable and worthwhile.
  - It is possible to achieve my goal.
  - The steps I need to carry out in order to achieve my goal are ecological and appropriate.
  - I have all the necessary abilities to achieve my goal.
  - I deserve to achieve my goal.

- After considering these statements review your responses, then ask:
    - What do I need to work on?
    - What can I do about it?
    - Am I willing to change that particular belief?

BEING AWARE OF INVISIBLES: EXERCISES

1. Use the Hierarchy of Values exercise covered in the section.
2. Listen out for types of language used when learners are talking about values and beliefs.
3. Use the outcomes process to help learners focus in their beliefs as this may well bring out 'can't' or 'won't' language.
4. Use mental rehearsal, visualization, affirmative techniques, get learners to do so.
5. Use the NLP systemic belief approach.
6. Use sub-modalities to establish structure of values and beliefs (consider using wishing to wanting process). (See 4.24 Using sub-modalities, page 186.)
7. Use timelines to establish and deal with the time any limiting decision was first made, and/or to put the new belief into your timeline. (See 4.19 Using timelines, page 162.)
8. Use Meta Programs to establish whether you are moving away/moving toward, etc. (See 4.21 Using Meta Programs, page 167.)

BEING AWARE OF INVISIBLES: KEY POINTS

☐ Be aware of the logical levels model and the questions that go with it.
☐ Recognize that environments, behaviour and some capabilities are visible.
☐ Recognize that some capabilities, values, beliefs and identity are invisible.
☐ Be aware of being perceived as attacking the invisibles.
☐ Remember that learners will often use vague language when talking about the invisibles.
☐ Use NLP techniques to establish logical levels.
☐ Use the Hierarchy of Values exercise to establish beliefs, etc about training, learning, etc.
☐ Use systemic beliefs approach to bring about change.

4.9 CREATING REFERENCE EXPERIENCES

For learning to be effective it must create a compelling experience. These are known as either reference experiences or significant emotional events.

Most people have had examples of significant emotional events in their lives and many of them may have been negative, for example redundancy, bereavement, divorce. Equally, they may have been positive, getting married, success at work or in a hobby. In other words they are events that change people's lives and/or their views on life. Training can create a positive reference experience.

The key point is that reference experiences normally impact at the higher levels of the logical levels model, ie values, beliefs, identity (see page 127). Many of us will know people whose whole view of the world has changed after a dramatic loss or a particularly positive experience.

The aim, therefore, is to create positive reference experiences for learners which will be important to them on a number of levels. As a trainer it is always intriguing and encouraging when people tell you long after a course that something that was said or done had enormous significance for them and will never be forgotten.

What is intriguing is the variety of ways that positive reference experiences can be created for learners. Everything that is covered in this book could be the key reference experience for an individual learner, from any 'off the cuff' comment you have forgotten you made, to the outcome from a major all-day training exercise.

From experience of the variety of strategies and techniques covered in this book the key areas likely to create reference experiences are:

- styles of training;
- creating rapport;
- using anchors;
- maintaining a positive personal state (and allowing them to as well);
- getting participants to set own goals (many of them are not used to this and don't expect it);
- using language patterns;
- using embedded commands;
- being aware of invisibles – values, beliefs and identity;
- creating new learning patterns;
- creating personal flexibility;
- working in both brain hemisphere functions;
- using sub-modalities;
- using Meta Programs;
- using timelines.

One key point regarding reference experiences is that for them to work to maximum benefit they should impact on learners in all the main representation systems, ie visual, auditory and kinesthetic. This also allows for the learners, either consciously or unconsciously, to anchor the experience for themselves.

In order to build up a library of reference experiences it can be useful to ask people at the end of each session/day what three things made the greatest impact on them that session/day.

While, as shown in the list above, there may be patterns in terms of what works best for learners, as soon as trainers feel that they 'know' what will work for learners, they may well lose some flexibility and the ability to impact appropriately, across the full spectrum.

CREATING REFERENCE EXPERIENCES: EXERCISES

1. Use any of the skills and techniques covered in this book, eg creating rapport, using anchors, using language patterns, using timelines, using sub-modalities, using Meta Programs.
2. Find out from learners their worst thoughts regarding learning in general or the particular topic you are on:
   - get them to visualize loving it, engaging it and finding it worthwhile;
   - anchor new feeling;
   - future pace.
3. Get learners to use outcomes process to help them move the reference experience on into the 'real world'.

CREATING REFERENCE EXPERIENCES: KEY POINTS

- ☐ Learners will have had reference experiences in other aspects of their lives.
- ☐ Reference experiences tend to impact at the higher logical levels, ie values, beliefs and identity, then drive down and affect capabilities, behaviour and environment.
- ☐ Learner reference experiences should be positive.
- ☐ Any part of the training experience is potentially a reference experience.
- ☐ Any of the NLP techniques can create a reference experience.
- ☐ Reference experiences should impact in the three main representation systems, ie visual, auditory and kinesthetic.
- ☐ Build up a library of reference experiences, by asking learners.
- ☐ Always stay flexible and willing to try any purposeful route to achieving reference experiences.

CREATING REFERENCE EXPERIENCES: CASE STUDY

A participant on a management development programme was very open about his disempowering beliefs regarding his ability to command attention and get people to listen to him. At work he was being considered for a promotion, because of his technical skills, but was very wary about accepting it.

During the programme the other group members became stuck in carrying out a complex task and started to unravel as a group. Despite not understanding the task in question, but based on the teamwork skills taught on the programme, the individual stepped in, took the lead and the issue was resolved.

Afterwards he received positive, specific feedback from the other delegates. When the trainer asked him what had prompted him to do it, he responded that he couldn't see the group fail and had forgotten about his own perceived limitations.

As a consequence, he accepted the job on offer and now, four years on, has been promoted again, and still refers back to the experience above as the key event that made him believe in himself.

4.10 CREATING NEW LEARNING PATTERNS

Many people arrive on training courses or into education generally, having acquired or adopted a particular learning style. Section 1.1, Styles of training (see page 11), mentions from the USA the Kolb 'Learning Styles Inventory' and from the UK the Peter Honey/Alan Mumford 'Learning Styles Questionnaire' (LSQ).

Particularly in the UK much work has taken place using the Honey/Mumford LSQ with regard to relating results to job types, eg accountants, production managers, and also to pointing out that no one style is wrong or right, but that flexibility can be an added strength. Most trainers in the UK will be aware of, and almost certainly have used in some way, the results of this work.

It can be useful in designing training programmes to be aware of the preferred learning styles of the attendees and then design the training appropriately. Even if this cannot be done, awareness and sensitivity while the training is actually taking place will be revealing as to what is working and what is not, eg whether it is due to inappropriate choice of content and/or materials, or possibly a mismatch between materials and the learning styles of the attendees.

Most trainers would recognize that, for example, in running an outdoor activity programme it may well be the Activists who make most of the running, want to lead from the front and not get too bogged down analysing what worked and what did not afterwards. Having said that the learning that the Activists can get, from either recognizing the skills and needs of the Reflectors, Theorists and Pragmatists or developing skills in learning using the other three styles where appropriate, can be of vital importance, because they can then take those skills and apply them in other situations.

CREATING NEW LEARNING PATTERNS: CASE STUDY

A production manager who attended an outdoor activity course received lots of information and feedback on the benefits and issues of his predominantly Activist styles. Like many people on training courses (particularly Activists!) he then saw it as 'the meaning of life' and wanted to apply it to everything, whether it was appropriate or not.

One situation where he had received adverse comments at work but did not know how to respond, was his conduct in meetings. His tendency was to jump in, interrupt others and force his own point of view, with total disregard for anyone else. In doing this he was also able to upset and alienate any other Activists who were attending the meeting.

Through working with the guidelines he had received with the LSQ plus some one-to-one coaching he was able to work on modifying his behaviour and increase his impact and effectiveness in meetings.

The key issue in this story is that sometimes it is part of the role of the trainer to help learners develop or create new learning patterns. Occasionally, this can involve instructing people, sometimes challenging them as to the appropriateness of their style, and sometimes allowing them to find their own best way to increase their flexibility. The previously mentioned notes (see page 11), that are part of Peter Honey and Alan Mumford's LSQ, are an invaluable aid to help people should they chose to increase their skill base into new learning pattern areas.

The other advantage that this information can provide is an explanation as to why they may have found some types of learning and education difficult. For example, a reflector who is trying to learn something new in a situation where there isn't sufficient time to ponder, think and absorb everything that is going on may well feel stressed and uncomfortable.

They may also think it's their own fault, ie that they are stupid, or stuck, or just can't get the hang of it, but in reality it may be the mismatch between the style they prefer and the style being used. If we create situations where people think it must be their fault we are not aiding our cause. Using the skills of NLP will allow trainers to develop their own flexibility and respond more effectively for the learner.

Another learning pattern known as the 4 MAT system is used mainly in the USA; developed by Bernice McCarthy it is based on the work of David

Kolb. This breaks learning styles down into four types of learner, and creates a framework for covering all four types by anticipating their preferences, needs and the key questions they will ask.

The opening questions each type will want answering are:

Style	Question
Diverger	Why are we doing the training?
Assimilator	What are we going to do?
Converger	How are we going to cover it?
Accommodator	What if? How can it be used?

These questions have also been covered in 4.5 Changing learner states (page 120).

Therefore the trainer introducing a topic on a course needs to answer all the questions in the order of: Why? What? How? What if? in order to ensure that all attendees can relate to what is going to take place.

Based on the work of Bernice McCarthy issues that need to be recognized regarding these styles are:

Diverger

People with this learning style are best at receiving concrete information from many different points of view. Their approach to situations is to observe rather than take action. They enjoy situations that call for generating a wide range of ideas such as brainstorming sessions. They probably have broad cultural interests and like to gather information. The imaginative ability and sensitivity to feelings is useful in arts, entertainment and service careers.

Assimilator

People with this learning style are best at understanding a wide range of information and putting it into concise, logical form. They are probably less focused on people and more interested in abstract ideas and concepts. For example, they find it more important that a theory has logical soundness than practical values. This is important for effectiveness in information and science careers.

Converger

People with this learning style are best at finding practical uses for ideas and theories. They have the ability to solve problems and make decisions based on finding solutions to questions or problems. They would rather deal with technical tasks and problems than with social and interpersonal issues. These leaning styles are important for effectiveness in specialist and technology careers.

Accommodator

People with this learning style have the ability to learn primarily from hands-on experience. They probably enjoy carrying out plans and involving themselves in new and challenging experiences. The tendency may be to act on gut feeling rather than logical analysis. In solving problems they rely more heavily on people for information than on their own technical analysis. This can be important for effectiveness in action-oriented careers such as marketing or sales.

An overview of the strengths, weaknesses and ideas for developing flexibility are:

Diverger
Strengths: Imaginative ability, understanding people, recognizing problems, brainstorming.
Weaknesses: Paralysed by alternatives, can't make decisions.
Actions to develop Diverger skills: Being sensitive to people, listening with open mind, being sensitive to values.

Assimilator
Strengths: Planning, creating models, defining problems, developing theories.
Weaknesses: Castles in the air, impractical applications, unable to learn from mistakes, no systematic approach.
Actions to develop Assimilator skills: Build conceptual models, test theories/models, design experiments, analyse data.

Converger
Strengths: Problem solving, decision making, deductive reasoning, defining problems.
Weaknesses: Solving wrong problems, hasty decision maker, lack of focus, scattered thoughts.
Actions to develop Converger skills: Creating new ideas, experimenting, setting goals, making decisions.

Accommodator
Strengths: Getting things done, leadership, risk taking.
Weaknesses: Meaningless activity, work not completed on time, impractical plans, not directed to goals.
Actions to develop Accommodator skills: Committing to objectives, seeking new opportunities, influencing and leading, dealing with people.

Based upon figures developed in the USA, the population is divided into:

Diverger	35%
Assimilator	18%
Converger	22%
Accommodator	25%

In some learning circumstances, when a number of Divergers have been sent, it will be vital to answer the often unspoken 'Why?' question for them. This will mean pointing out the benefits, asking questions such as 'would it be helpful to...?'; 'let me show you a consequence of...'. The more hostile the audience the more important to ask, and answer, the likely question. The key point in creating new learning patterns is to cycle through all four stages of the model, to cover all the important issues for all the styles.

CREATING NEW LEARNING PATTERNS: EXERCISES

1. Use any of the relevant skills and techniques, eg future pacing, being aware of invisibles, Meta Programs to help learners create new patterns.
2. Use mental preparation, affirmation.
3. Get groups of learners to play with different ways to learn, then, if helpful, either anchor and future pace or agree an outcome.
4. Get learners into groups of four and get them to discuss 'how we would encourage other people to create new learning patterns' then each group repeats back, shares and each individual establishes a new learning outcome.
5. Get learners to establish sub-modalities (see 4.24 Using sub-modalities, page 186) for various current learning patterns. Examples could be:
   - How do you prefer to study?
   - How do you motivate yourself to learn?
   - How do you prepare to write a report?
   - How do you prefer to learn?

CREATING NEW LEARNING PATTERNS: KEY POINTS

☐ Use Peter Honey and Alan Mumford's 'Learning Styles Questionnaire'.
☐ Use Kolb's 'Learning Styles Inventory'.
☐ Remember the relationship of patterns to certain job types.
☐ If possible, design training programmes to match, then stretch learners.
☐ Use the 4 Mat system.
☐ Answer the why? what? how? what if? questions.
☐ Help learners develop greater flexibility and new patterns.
☐ Use all four stages of the model.

4.11 NOTICING BEHAVIOURAL CHANGES

It may well sound obvious to say that the trainer should be perceptive enough to notice and, if appropriate, respond to behavioural changes, but often two things occur. One is that the trainer, for whatever reason, fails to pick up signals because the change, although evident, is a small one. This may be due to the trainer wanting to see huge, step changes. Or the trainer picks up on the change before the learner and goes into overload in giving them the feedback and actually discouraging and demotivating the learner. This is rather like killing the baby with kindness.

The optimum strategy is to use the 'trainer state' and any other skills and techniques and to notice, without judging or interpreting, the change. Then by questions or sensory specific feedback help the learner recognize what has taken place, draw some conclusions from it and plan how to take it forward.

This doesn't necessarily have to be done formally or in open session. It can be done over coffee, walking along a corridor, or in the bar. Often the learner will ask the trainer for a reason or an answer to the behavioural change, or to decide whether it is 'right or wrong'. Sometimes this should be done but normally the trainer should resist the temptation and help the learner to their conclusions. Any behavioural change no matter how slight *may* be of enormous significance, but the advantage can be lost if the trainer is not perceptive enough to utilize the moment appropriately.

NOTICING BEHAVIOURAL CHANGES: EXERCISES

1. Use any of the relevant skills and techniques covered in this book, eg using non-verbal communication, using language patterns, being aware of invisibles.
2. Develop specific anchors and notice their effect on learners' behaviour.
3. Focus on something to work on, eg a specific input to be delivered, or the 'self-talk internal dialogue', or the non-verbal communication, or on the language patterns you use. Notice how this affects your own behaviour and how this affects learners' behaviour as well.
4. Use this exercise to help develop a new behaviour for yourself:
   - Think of something you would like to believe about yourself but don't really think is true, eg being confident in giving a presentation, impacting well on people on first acquaintance.
   - Check the belief required by putting it through the outcomes process.
   - Think of what someone with the belief required would naturally do. List the actions.
   - Think of a future time when you would like to have the required belief in place.
   - Choose two actions from your list that would be helpful and appropriate.
   - Visualize yourself (disassociated) doing this as if in a film.
   - Run the film again but this time step in and become fully associated, notice all the VAKOG senses that accompany this. Speak your new belief and behaviour out loud.
   - Repeat five to ten times.
   - Repeat twice daily or as long as is required.

NOTICING BEHAVIOURAL CHANGES: KEY POINTS

☐ Pick up on all signals offered.
☐ Avoid going into overload on feedback.
☐ Use the trainer state.
☐ Use questions.
☐ Use sensory specific feedback, if feedback is required.
☐ Help learner find own conclusions.
☐ Use informal opportunities to discuss.
☐ Avoid giving judgement on right or wrong.
☐ Anchor and/or future pace.

4.12 USING EFFECTIVE FEEDBACK

Using effective feedback has obviously been around since long before the development of NLP. But, like many other aspects of good practice, it fits in and follows all the key principles.

As stated in the previous section on noticing behavioural changes, there is often a decision to be made by the trainer, which is: (a) whether to actually give the feedback, and (b) if so, how to do it for maximum effectiveness.

It is worth bearing in mind that just diving in regardless can sometimes do more harm than good. Providing that feedback is appropriate the following 'sandwich' approach is very useful, and is based upon sound NLP principles:

(a) Give sensory specific, positive feedback based on a strength, supported by actual examples.
(b) Give sensory specific feedback based on a weakness, supported by actual examples.
(c) Give, or open out, by using questions, a positive direction ahead, but one determined by the receiver in regard to their specific actions.

In order for the feedback to be of maximum use to the receiver it should be as close to the actual event as possible. The further away from the event, the more likely that a distortion factor will have occurred which will blur the edges and it can be quite easy to find you are talking about the issues associated with the event, and what has happened since, rather than moving forward. This will become apparent in the amount of Meta Model violations that occur in discussing the incident.

In its simplest terms, using the feedback sandwich means providing someone with useful information to help them determine their subsequent behaviour, but the information is sensory specific rather than subjective or judgemental. Some trainers are reluctant to ask others to change their behaviour because they are afraid they might hurt the receiver, or make them angry or dislike them, or cause them to argue or retaliate in some defensive, disagreeable way. That's probably because most people get defensive when they are criticized, even if the giver thinks that criticism is 'constructive'. NLP allows us to avoid this problem by being sensory specific.

But feedback is not the same as 'constructive criticism' or advice giving. With the latter, the one offering the criticism or advice is taking responsibility for deciding what to do. Therein lies the major difference. With feedback, only information is given, and the person receiving the feedback is responsible for the decision about what to do. The other differences are:

- Criticism focuses on the person, where as feedback focuses on the behaviour or the situation.
- Criticism is general and conclusive, but feedback is specific.
- Criticism is evaluative, blaming and fault finding, while feedback is descriptive and remedy seeking.
- Criticism dwells on what happened, the past; feedback emphasizes what will be done, the future.
- Criticism is often saved up, feedback is timely.

The outcome of criticizing someone is generally resentment and the feeling of being punished. The outcome of feedback is usually cooperation and movement toward change. We tend to think of feedback mainly in relation to undesirable behaviour (negative feedback). But the feedback sandwich principles can and should apply to desirable behaviour (positive feedback) as well. Remember that in NLP there is no failure, there is only feedback.

Some classic responses to feedback are:

Positive
Listen carefully, acknowledge, clarify, check, evaluate, incorporate, observe, further.

Negative
Ignore, deny, explain, justify, excuse, project, resist, defend, distort, fight, surrender, forget.

Therefore effective feedback is information that:

- can be heard by the learner without the learner becoming defensive;
- keeps the relationship healthy, open and intact;
- validates the feedback process in future interactions.

Effective feedback

- describes the behaviour;
- is sensory specific;
- comes as seems appropriate;
- is direct;
- is owned by the sender;
- includes sender's real feeling;
- is checked for clarity;
- asks relevant questions;
- specifies consequences;
- is solicited or desired;
- refers to behaviours which are under receiver's control;
- takes into account both sender's and receiver's needs;
- affirms the receiver's worth;
- acknowledges process.

Ineffective feedback

- evaluates and judges the behaviour;
- is general;
- is delayed, saved up;
- is indirect, or vague;
- transfers ownership;
- denies feelings;
- is not checked for clarity;
- asks questions which are irrelevant;
- has vague or unspecified consequences;
- is unsolicited or imposed;
- refers to behaviours which are not under receiver's control;
- is distorted by the sender's needs;
- denies the receiver's worth;
- ignores process.

Giving positive feedback

Many trainers understand the value of praise and recognition (positive feedback) but have found it difficult to balance with negative feedback. One of the most important lessons for trainers to be learned from NLP and psychology is the role of positive reinforcement. It appears to be a much more powerful motivation than negative reinforcement. While continuous negative reinforcement may result in short-term lapse of an undesirable behaviour, it usually won't inspire good performance. In fact, it may produce strange, unpredictable, behavioural change.

In many instances, trainers feel uncomfortable giving feedback because they don't know how to say what they really mean. They can't seem to find the right words to express how they genuinely feel. Often it comes out as 'yes, er, well done'.

Regardless of how it is said, such brevity is unlikely to convey the true meaning or intent of the trainer. NLP with its range of skills and techniques provides useful tools to help the trainer assist the learner even more effectively. There are three ways to add strength and meaning to positive feedback.

- Be specific.
- Reinforce a personal quality.
- Emphasize the payoffs.

By being specific the trainer adds depth to what might otherwise appear an off hand remark. For example, if giving positive feedback to someone about a question they have just asked, the trainer could say:

'I particularly like the way you had thought the question through in a step-by-step, logical way.'

'You asked the question in a clear, direct way.'

'The part regarding future applications was really clear and hard hitting.'

This doesn't require the use of NLP jargon, but does allow the learner to receive precise feedback and, by being specific, the trainer leaves a lasting impression that she really means what she is saying. This, coupled with the rapport, calibration, appropriate use of language patterns, creates something the receiver can purposefully respond to.

Often there are underlying factors that stimulate a learner's good performance. A few of these intangible factors are: patience, perseverance, attention to detail, tactfulness, thoroughness, and other qualities that are woven into the very fabric of an individual's personality. If the trainer values these personal qualities and wants people to continue to exhibit them, they should be reinforced through positive feedback, focused on the behaviour.

Some examples of reinforcing a personal quality are:

'I'm glad you took the initiative.'

'You were firm but fair.'

'That's a very creative approach.'

Many people, particularly those who are results oriented, like to know that what they are doing has purpose or value. The third method for adding substance to positive feedback is to emphasize the payoffs. Tell the learner how you or the organization, or the other learners, or the customer or client would benefit from their use of that particular skill, eg:

'The others in the group were helped by that question.'
'You really helped me explain the past more effectively by asking that question.'

Choose whatever words are comfortable and appropriate. But when giving positive feedback, be specific, reinforce a personal quality, and/or emphasize payoffs. When all three are put together, it might sound like this:

'I'm glad you were sensitive to the possible misunderstanding and asked the question to double check. It could have been an embarrassing situation.'

This has the benefit of being specific and allows the learner to focus on the key points. It avoids mind reading or commenting on whether other people approved or not.

Giving negative feedback

It is obviously important to be able to give positive feedback for something you value. But what about bad news? How can a trainer call attention to an error or a failure in a way that is seen as constructive and supportive? It's not easy, and it can arouse defensiveness. But helping people learn from their mistakes is an important aspect of building and maintaining a motivational climate. It's also extremely important in the context of the trainer as a role-model. How can a trainer ensure that they 'walk the talk' and live out the NLP operating principles in a demonstrable way? The following step-by-step process will help to reduce the defensiveness and turn a potentially unpleasant situation into collaborative problem solving and positive change. The steps are:

- Express your concern.
- Understand the whole story.
- Use NLP sensory skills.
- Reinforce correct performance.
- Discuss alternatives.
- Help learner develop own outcome.

Clear and open communication is a prerequisite. That's why it is important to begin the process by carefully and thoroughly explaining what's on your mind. Use 'I messages' like:

'I've noticed the lack of involvement...'
'I'm concerned about...'
'I have a problem with...'

Avoid opening with a question or anything that may sound like a judgement or accusation. Questions like 'Can't you keep up with the others?' or 'Where were you when this lesson started?' only seem to increase defensiveness and anxiety. Be tactful, but be direct. If you are too subtle, you may create confusion and doubt. Once you've expressed your concern, immediately follow up with a question that invites explanation:

'What happened?'
'Why was it done that way?'
'Tell me about it.'

If appropriate the trainer can use the Meta Model, but should recognize that the aim is to move the learner forward, not just get to the bottom of a particular situation, although it is vital to understand the issue thoroughly in order to act in a constructive way.

Key steps are:

- Listening carefully – watch physiology, eye accessing cues, listen for language patterns.
- Asking clarifying questions – using Meta Model.
- Confirming understanding, even though it is not always possible to agree with the person.

Try useful phrases like:

'What you are saying is...'
'Then the reason you...'

Genuine listening is a vital ingredient in all effective communication, and that is one way that using NLP skills will convey genuine listening to the learner. Often it is possible to discover that behind a poor performance were the best of intentions. If so, it's important to reinforce the good parts of the performance so that you can focus solutions on the error or misjudgement. Otherwise the learner is likely to assume both the reason and the action were inappropriate or incorrect.

For example, suppose some written work contained several errors because the learner thought it was more important to get the work in to a given deadline. Reinforcing the learner's concern for timeliness will help preserve this quality while seeking solutions to the issue of accuracy.

Having expressed the concern, listened to, and understood, the whole story and focused on the issue by reinforcing positive results already achieved, the next stage is to discuss alternative ways to handle the situation next time it occurs. This is the fourth step in the process for negative feedback. It's important because it takes the positive past issues and looks constructively toward the future.

There are two ways to approach this step of the process. If the intention is to draw out the other person's idea, or if you cannot think of any other alternatives of your own, you can ask for possible solutions. If you have a suggestion yourself, or if there is only one course of action open, make the suggestion. Don't try to 'lead' the other person to a solution that you consider to be useful by asking a series of questions. Learners are likely to become resentful of such a manipulative technique. Use creating rapport and other appropriate NLP techniques. Also help them move towards defining an outcome of their own.

Here is how it might sound:

'It was a tight deadline, and I appreciate the extra effort it took to get the written work to me on time. What can be done to reduce the number of errors and still hit the deadline?'

Accurate, timely and genuine feedback is one of the keystones of being an effective trainer. Praise and recognition become more meaningful when they are specific, reinforce personal qualities and emphasize payoffs. Even negative feedback is seen as supportive when the process is based upon open, two-way communication and constructive problem solving.

How to give feedback

1. Use 'I' statements to describe reactions. Avoid 'you' statements which evaluate the other person.
   'I was uncomfortable when you said that' *not* 'you make me feel uncomfortable'.
2. Comment on a specific situation or behaviour.
   'When Jane mentioned the cost, I thought you looked upset' *not* 'You took Jane all wrong'.
3. Make sure the comments serve a need for the learner. Be careful not to address just your our needs.
   'It seemed like you were angry' *not* 'I was irritated to see you react so angrily. I've always felt you were very short tempered'.
4. Give feedback only when it can effect change. Avoid giving feedback on things over which the learner has no control.
   'Your volume was so low that the people in the back of the room could hardly hear' *not* 'Because you were quiet most people did not pay attention to your comments'.
5. Avoid mixed messages, eg:
   'I've gathered some complaints from the people on the course. You're upsetting them a bit. But your questions in open session are excellent.'
6. Don't use questions that ask learners to justify their actions.
   'Can you tell me about it?' *not* 'Why did you do that?'
7. Avoid overload, eg:
   'You've got to get here on time. We also have a problem with you in the groups. Don't forget about your presentation later today.'

One final point: should you as a trainer ever hear the words 'you know what I mean' forming in your head, think again, the learner won't. It's a shorthand that achieves compliance with a knee-jerk nod, but does not really address the issue.

The length of this section emphasizes how vital the skill of giving feedback is for the effective trainer and, as we said at the beginning, effective feedback predates the formal development of NLP. But NLP is pragmatic and based upon what works and, therefore, there is a complementary fit. In order for feedback to be effective, fitting in with NLP skills and principles will be of enormous benefit.

USING EFFECTIVE FEEDBACK: EXERCISES

1. Use all the relevant skills when giving feedback, eg creating rapport, pacing and leading, using language patterns, using Meta Programs to ensure feedback is effective.
2. Match learners' preferences rather than use own.
3. Ask learners for feedback including asking them what was effective feedback for them (notice their eye accessing cues, non-verbals, language patterns). This creates a complete training loop.

USING EFFECTIVE FEEDBACK: KEY POINTS

☐ Decide whether to give feedback.
☐ Decide how to do it for maximum effectiveness.
☐ Use the feedback sandwich.
☐ Give feedback as soon as possible after the event.
☐ Use sensory specific language and examples.
☐ Follow key NLP principles.
☐ Leave decision regarding feedback to the learner.
☐ Use information that:
　　– can be heard without causing defensiveness;
　　– keeps relationship healthy, open and intact;
　　– validates the feedback process.
☐ Use criteria for effective feedback.
☐ In giving positive feedback:
　　– be specific;
　　– reinforce on personal quality;
　　– emphasize the payoffs.
☐ In giving negative feedback:
　　– express the concern;
　　– understand the whole story;

- use NLP sensory skills;
- reinforce correct performance;
- discover alternatives;
- help learner develop own outcome.

☐ Use the key steps:
  - Listen carefully – watch physiology, eye accessing cues, listen for language patterns.
  - Ask clarifying questions – use Meta Model.
  - Confirm understanding, even though it is not always possible to agree with the person.

☐ Use the key rules:
  - Use 'I' not 'you' language.
  - Discuss specific situation on behaviour.
  - Ensure comments serve needs of the learner.
  - Only give feedback when it can effect change.
  - Avoid mixed messages.
  - Don't use questions that ask learners to justify their actions.
  - Avoid overload.

GIVING FEEDBACK: CASE STUDY

Following an exercise in a team building workshop, which had gone wrong, with embarrassment all round, a manager approached the trainer to ask for feedback.

By listening to the question, how it was asked, and calibrating to the individual, the trainer thought that it was actually advice that was being sought, but also that the questioner would not receive the advice in an open way and would probably fight and resist it.

Therefore, rather than actually give feedback she decided to ask questions, using the Meta Model to look for violations to establish the real issue.

In doing this it became apparent that the manager felt that he had made a fool of himself and not handled himself in the way he thought he should have.

Having exposed the real issue, the trainer then by being aware of values and beliefs, and using reframing and artfully vague language, combined with anchoring voice tones, enabled the manager to choose a specific course of action decided by himself, which he then went off and did.

Later on in the workshop the manager commented to the trainer that, although the trainer hadn't actually done anything, the manager felt that he had learnt something useful about himself, which he would carry on working towards.

4.13 UNSTICKING PEOPLE

The reasons that people become 'stuck' can be many and varied, ranging from fatigue, boredom, overload, poor quality training, environmental issues, lack of interest in the topic. Therefore, it is vital that the trainer is able to 'fine-tune' both individuals and groups in order to recognize what is taking place and deal appropriately with it. All of the NLP sensory and language skills come into play to great effect at this point.

All of the techniques covered in this book will, if used appropriately, help to move people on. Sometimes there is a tendency to ease up or slow down if a group seems to be finding a topic difficult. A more effective strategy is not only to keep groups active and busy but to ensure that both the left and right brain functions are being employed, but also *challenged*. Therefore the most effective way to move people forward is to engage the brain at another level while at the same time reaffirming previous successes. One significant piece of research carried out by Bandura (1986) at Stanford University indicated that the brain releases different chemicals when feeling stressed to when it feels capable and confident.

This research was followed up by Athern and Schwartz at Yale University in 1987 who found that when people were feeling low, unmotivated or depressed, the right side of the brain was most activated (Maguire, 1990). Alternatively, when people were optimistic about events the left brain was most activated.

Another aspect of 'unsticking' people relates to the personal skills of the trainer. As well as using a wide variety of training techniques, the trainer needs to be open enough to recognize that trainees are learning at an unconscious level. In fact, Dr Donchin at the University of Illinois states that 99 per cent of all learning is unconscious (reported in Jensen, 1994a). Trainees learn from visual cues, sounds, experiences, the environment. Therefore, effective trainers will see themselves as part of the learning environment and be prepared to be flexible.

This could involve changing subjects, stopping completely, using a variety of voice tonalities and speed, changing the language patterns being used, using humour, getting learners to have a short (one minute) nonsense conversation with each other, asking them for the most offbeat idea for moving forward, using exercise bursts, asking for or creating a state change, using props.

In order for these techniques to succeed they need to be based upon mutual respect built upon strong rapport. All of these techniques will work but doing them 'just for effect' can produce a boomerang response whereby the trainer 'sticks' people even more, or creates a team dynamic within the group by excluding themselves from it. Used properly they engage attention, redirect focus and re-energize individuals and groups. They also allow for establishing positive anchors and future pacing for events inside and outside the learning event.

UNSTICKING PEOPLE: EXERCISES

1. Use any of the relevant skills and techniques covered in this book, eg being aware of invisibles, creating reference experiences, changing learner states, etc. Virtually all NLP techniques can be used to unstick people individually or collectively.
2. Practise using NLP techniques to unstick self.

UNSTICKING PEOPLE: KEY POINTS

☐ Stay outwardly focused on individuals and the group.
☐ Use the techniques covered in this section of the book.
☐ Engage and challenge people.
☐ Engage both sides of the brain.
☐ Be aware of optimistic left brain.
☐ Build on capabilities and confidence.
☐ Be a good role-model.
☐ Be flexible and willing to try different things.
☐ Create rapport before changing direction.
☐ If it is not possible to create rapport before changing direction – change the direction anyway as this will interrupt the stuck state *but* always lead to a positive direction, use anchors and future pace.

4.14 USING REVERSE TESTS

In traditional education the idea of tests provokes debate and often controversy. Everyone has an opinion (supported by some very strong beliefs) regarding the rights and wrongs of using tests. This presents an interesting opportunity for the trainer. Recognizing the often negative implications of tests and turning that round by making them fun, useful and interesting can provide a major breakthrough (even a reference experience) for a lot of people.

One way to start this process is to get the learners to 'test' the trainer. If expectations or objectives have been agreed at the beginning of the training, then at key points, eg just before a break or part way through a session (to help create energy and group dynamics) the trainer can show a flipchart of what they are trying to achieve and how they are trying to achieve it. The learners can then either comment on it, or complete a one page scoring on the trainer, which is then fed back to the whole group, thus creating a training loop.

Based upon the work of Eric Jensen (1994a) an example would be:

- What (if anything) makes the course useful?
- What is the trainer doing to help me achieve my objectives?
- What more (or less) could the trainer do to help me achieve my objectives?
- What do you think of the handouts, visual aids etc?
- What I still don't understand is.....
- What feedback would you give the trainer?
- What marks out of ten would you give the trainer at this point in the training?
- Does the trainer actually live out and demonstrate the skills being taught?

If the trainer has set out to train in a certain way they can design their own test and ask the learners to give them feedback. An example could be:

Using a scale of 1–10 rate the trainer on the following topics.

1. Listens and understands.
2. Planned the session well.
3. Enthusiastic regarding the topic.
4. Enthusiastic regarding the group.
5. Materials are up to date.
6. Willing to change mind.
7. Ran to schedule.
8. Allowed enough time for discussion.

Obviously some trainers would be wary of doing this, while others would say that they already do something similar, eg the evaluation at the end of a programme. The key point here is that this approach should be carried out on a regular ongoing basis, with questions being asked geared to the specific session being taught and/or how it's being taught.

Having done this the trainer then needs to be able to respond to the results of the tests and demonstrate behavioural change and flexible skills. This provides a strong model for the learners to follow.

Another form of using reverse tests is getting the learners to design their own tests by themselves for themselves. The steps for this process are as follows.

- Split the group into fours.
- Remind them of objectives.
- Give them a quick overrun of content.
- Get them to design a ten-question test.
- Share results in an open session.

- Agree final test.
- Carry out test.
- Discuss validity of test.

This process again creates a complete training loop.

Regarding the skills covered in the book, trainers can test themselves on specific skills, eg creating rapport, using humour, changing learner states, using pre-suppositions. Whatever skills are tested will also help embed them for the learners as well.

USING REVERSE TESTS: EXERCISES

1. Design your own test for learners to complete based on objectives/expectations agreed.
2. Get learners to design tests for themselves to be carried out by themselves.
3. Base tests (if appropriate) on key NLP skills.

USING REVERSE TESTS: KEY POINTS

☐ Reverse tests can help change any negative views learners have regarding tests.
☐ They create a complete training loop.
☐ The trainer receives useful, immediate feedback.
☐ The trainer can demonstrate a response.
☐ The quality of the training can be improved.
☐ They should be carried out on a regular basis, eg daily (but at a different time each day).
☐ Learners can develop their own tests.
☐ Skills can (and should) be tested as well as knowledge.

USING REVERSE TESTS: CASE STUDY

In running a two-day influencing skills workshop the trainer decided to use a reverse test at the end of day one. One of the questions was 'Does the trainer live out the skills he is training?'

The feedback to this question indicated that he did, with the exception of creating rapport, because he didn't always pick up on the underlying themes the learners were getting at.

This feedback enabled him to change his approach and on day two behaviourally demonstrate that he could do it. This allowed the group to get more from the training and also show them that behavioural change was achievable.

4.15 MAINTAINING INVOLVEMENT

This, as all trainers know, is a vital element in all trainings and everyone has their own way of achieving it. Every NLP skill covered in this book will aid this process, from energy bursts through to Meta Programs.

In the early stages of using NLP skills it can be a little daunting as the trainer is even more aware of what is happening. It seems as though every blink, swallow or gesture conveys enormous significance (often perceived as negative by the trainer). The important point to remember is that everyone has their own way of doing things (which almost certainly won't be our way). As long as it is working for them, then it is working for us as well. If for some reason it isn't working, the trainer, using the appropriate NLP skills, can help the learner get back on track.

The trainer can also set out to develop certain NLP skills to help create and then maintain involvement, eg creating rapport, changing learner states, using perceptual positions, using reframing, using sub-modalities. The important issue is that the trainer has the flexibility to choose, possibly based on feedback received in using reverse tests.

Another way is just to ask learners directly, eg:

● How many of you are/were really involved in this session?
● Of those of you that did not feel involved, what else can I do to help you stay involved?
● What else can you do to maintain your own involvement?

Again the use of NLP skills will help the trainer get high quality feedback, not just verbally, while helping maintain involvement for the learners.

MAINTAINING INVOLVEMENT: EXERCISES

1. Chose specific NLP skills to work on, practise using the exercises covered in that section.
2. Specifically practise maintaining a positive personal state when asking the questions, receiving the feedback.
3. Ask the learners direct questions.

MAINTAINING INVOLVEMENT: KEY POINTS

☐ All trainers have their own ways of doing this.
☐ In the early stages of using NLP skills the amount of feedback can be daunting.
☐ Providing it's working for the learner it should be working for the trainer as well.
☐ Use the full range of NLP skills and techniques.
☐ Chose specific NLP skills to use/practise.
☐ Ask the learners directly for feedback.

4.16 INSTRUCTING PEOPLE

Many trainers today debate long and hard the role and amount of instructing that does, or should, take place. Oddly some trainers have found instructing harder to move away from than they imagined. This seems partly to do with the fear of losing control, which begs the question 'Who should be in control of the learning process in the first place?'

Obviously instructing can be the right approach to take in a training situation, but the evidence is that it can be over-used, or used inappropriately. One of the issues is the aspect of demonstrating a particular skill. Often trainers have stepped in when the learner is struggling, taken over the job themselves and frustrated and demotivated the learner even more. The consequence has been that the trainer has proven that they can do it, rather than helping the learner find out that they can.

Assuming that it is appropriate to instruct there are many ways that NLP can help, eg creating rapport, setting outcomes, using anchors, using perceptual positions, using big picture/little picture technique, using language patterns, using sleight of mouth, using embedded commands, changing learner states. Each of these, and many more, can help ensure that the quality of instruction is effective. Equally, of course, they can be used if a more flexible model of helping people learn is used.

INSTRUCTING PEOPLE: EXERCISES

1. Chose specific NLP skills to develop, eg
   - In using language patterns, listen for representation system and predicate preferences, match the pattern.
   - In using anchors, establish own and learner anchors for key learning points.
   - In using embedded commands, use a 'when' to make it clear to the learner that they will be able to do it using NLP skills.
2. Watch and listen for learners' preferences on how they do things.

INSTRUCTING PEOPLE: KEY POINTS

☐ Conventional instructing keeps the trainer in a form of control.
☐ Demonstrating the trainer's competence may not necessarily help the learner.
☐ NLP skills and techniques can be used to improve the quality of the instruction.

4.17 CREATING POSITIVE BELIEFS

As was the case for being aware of invisibles, eg values, beliefs and identities, this can be a very big issue for learners. NLP has achieved many breakthroughs in this area, and trainers who are interested in going further into this topic should follow up books mentioned in the Bibliography, particularly the work of Robert Dilts, or attend an NLP training. Some specific and developing areas relating NLP and beliefs are language, submodalities, timelines and Meta Programs. Further useful and exciting work remains to be done in all these areas.

One aspect of this is the 'belief' that some people have that beliefs are indelible, unchangeable and irreversible. As it says in the song it 'ain't necessarily so', and NLP has provided lots of ways to help address this. Any of the NLP processes can help achieve this and create reference experiences for learners which will help their learning both at the time and in the future. Creating reference experiences (see 4.9, page 129), mentions a number of situations that contribute to belief change, eg getting married, redundancy. The downside for many people is that it is the negative experience, eg bereavement, that has brought about the belief change.

Training can provide a powerful reference experience leading to positive belief change.

The importance of this becomes clear when considering the logical levels model covered earlier in this book (see Figure 4.3).

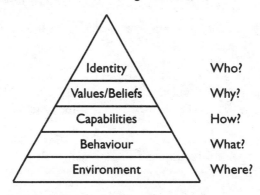

Figure 4.3 *Logical levels model – 1*

Many trainers and management thinkers who are involved in change at organizational and/or personal levels find that change may only be skin deep, ie that it is short term and only happens at a behaviour level. This can, of course, then move up to and become a new, changed and sustainable belief, *but often it doesn't*. Coming down the logical levels model means that it is the new or changed belief that is the driver, which means that any change is more likely to be owned by the organization or individual and, therefore, more permanent. In learning this can bring about enormous benefit and change.

One exercise that can be very powerful in assisting belief change is:

● Think of something about yourself (eg an aspect of learning) which you would like to believe, but you are not quite sure is true.
● Put it into an outcome frame answering all the key questions, eg
    – Positive?
    – Own part?
    – Specific?
    – Evidence?
    – Ecology?
    – Action?
● Consider what someone who had the desired belief would naturally and actually do. List these actions.
● Consider a time in the future when you would like to have this belief.
● Choose an action from your list that is evidence of the desired belief and would be appropriate for the specific future time and place you have chosen.
● Run a movie of yourself carrying out the action, do this four or five times – disassociated.
● Do this again, this time stepping inside and being part of it – associated, notice what you see, hear and feel. Say out loud your new belief.
● Repeat the previous two points a number of times.

You can also add in an extra step: repeat from the fifth point choosing a different action(s).

Note: This exercise begins to open out the 'How do I know what it is that I think I know' issue which can, particularly when related to other NLP techniques, really start to impact on creating positive beliefs.

It is also worth pointing out at this stage that this process, like some others in NLP, can look confusing, and even unnerving on paper. Carrying it out live is a lot easier than reading and trying to understand it in print.

CREATING POSITIVE BELIEFS: EXERCISES

1. Exercise 1 in Using reframing (page 83).
2. The systemic belief exercise covered in Being aware of invisibles (page 129).
3. Sub-modality exercises.
4. Meta Program exercises.
5. Timeline exercises.
6. The exercise covered within this section.
7. The SWISH exercise (page 192).
8. The new behaviour generator exercises (page 208).
9 The ten day challenge exercise (page 34).

CREATING POSITIVE BELIEFS: KEY POINTS

☐ Beliefs are key drives for capabilities and behaviours.
☐ Learners may have disempowering beliefs.
☐ NLP has majored in the field of beliefs.
☐ Beliefs can be changed.
☐ New beliefs can be created.
☐ Some change only takes place at the behavioural level and may be short term.
☐ There are many ways to work on beliefs.

4.18 ACCELERATED LEARNING

One observation stands out in regard to the impact of research into the brain and its preferred learning patterns – more has been learnt about the brain and how it performs in the last 15 years than at any other time in our history. Nowhere has this had more relevance than in accelerated learning and its application. Amazing results have been achieved in many different areas including sports, languages, education, business and language training.

Most of the research indicates that one of the reasons that accelerated learning has been proved to be so successful is its ease of use. Lots of the key principles applied have origins or connections with NLP and more developments and applications are likely in the next few years. A thorough grounding in accelerated learning is a vital part of the armoury of the effective trainer.

The key early figure in the development of accelerated learning is Georgi Lozanov, a Bulgarian doctor and psychiatrist. Most subsequent advancements are based to some degree or other on his work. His starting point was that most people had difficulty with various aspects of traditional learning. In fact he felt he had come up against a new medical condition caused by poor teaching methods. He called this 'didactogenic syndrome' and he blamed the poor results of normal teaching on this process (Lozanov, 1978, 1991).

In the late 1960s and early 1970s, astonishing claims were made for the results achieved in Bulgaria and other Eastern Bloc states, by Lozanov and his supporters. These claims caused mixed reactions around the world, but were of sufficient interest to get all sorts of people, institutes and other learning bodies, to investigate the claims, the steps used to achieve them and to see if similar results could be achieved in the West. Most of these early pioneers were based in America and by the late 1970s various societies were formed based in American universities.

This work, based on Lozanov's initial results, has been added to by various other sources, including applications of modern science, mental preparation used by many Olympic athletes and top sports stars, ancient Yoga and many others; and of course NLP.

The set of techniques which have now become the core of accelerated learning are now very well tried and tested, but also being developed all of the time. One of the key problems was that, although the early pioneers followed Lozanov's methods, they seemed to be unable to reproduce them to the same levels. This caused many people to doubt the validity of his results and to wonder if it wasn't all Soviet 'hype', a debate that rages to this day in education circles and has harmed many of the potential contributions accelerated learning could have made.

In order to maximize the potential benefits of using the accelerated learning approach it is important to have the essential building blocks in place. These are based on the work of Tad James and Wyatt Woodsmall (1988).

- Get learners motivated at the beginning.
- Get the information into the right size chunks.
- Put everything into a meaning and a context.
- Help learners to create a positive self-image.
- Create the right environment for learning.
- Put information into all representative systems.
- Make sure learners associate into the experience.
- Get learners to go inside and use internal, interactive visualization.
- Remember that mindless repetition of something is worse than useless.
- Use memory pegs to help embed.
- Use mnemonics to help embed.
- Use eye accessing cues.
- Use your own, and learners', sub-modalities.

Bearing these building blocks in mind the trainer can then start to follow the key techniques required to make accelerated learning effective. No specific knowledge of NLP is necessary, although as with all other aspects of this book, it would be of great benefit

The starting point in the process is to become aware of the balance of use of the representation systems:

- visual;
- auditory;
- kinesthetic;
- gustatory;
- olfactory.

This can be done by a combination of questioning, watching for eye accessing cues, listening to their language patterns, watching physiology. A short inventory questionnaire could also be developed in order to find out learners' preferences.

The model outlined here is taken from the Nightingale Conant Accelerated Learning package by Colin Rose and Brian Tracy (1995). This package is a very comprehensive approach to developing skills in this topic.

1. Create a resourceful mind.
2. Use multi-sensory intake.
3. Explain using the seven intelligences (see page 158).
4. Memorize the key elements.
5. Show you know.
6. Reflect.

Other key skills to aid the process of accelerated learning are as follows.

- Use the big picture/little picture technique.
- Use learning or mind maps.
- Break information down into smaller chunks.
- Stay in 'up time', ie concentrating and focused.
- Ask lots of questions of everyone.
- Work with a partner(s).
- Develop your own action checklists.
- Tick things off when completed.
- Read aloud.
- Put strong emphasis in your voice.
- Have a learning/training seat or posture.
- Use repeated, appropriate gestures at key points to embed information and create anchors.
- Use a highlighter pen for important points.

- Move around or shift position. Children often learn best while moving, then we make them stop and wonder why learning becomes harder and less fun.
- Use post-its and, once having captured all the issues, move them around into a workable shape.
- Visualize all over again, updating information.

An overview of the seven intelligences

The idea of seven intelligences is based on the work of Howard Gardner and his colleagues at Harvard University, and is based on three key factors.

1. Intelligence is not a fixed notion. No one is intelligent about everything, it may vary dependent on the situation.
2. Intelligence is a matter of skills and abilities. It's about what is done to achieve things.
3. People need to work to develop, use and improve their intelligence.

It is also important to remember that, although most learning is unconscious, it is possible to learn faster and to greater effect by using conscious processes (which may themselves become unconscious).

The other main factor that Howard Gardner points out is that traditional educators have tended to teach using left brain techniques based upon linguistic and mathematical intelligences. Therefore learning has been easier for those people with a natural skill for words and figures.

The seven intelligences are defined as:

- linguistic;
- mathematical/logical;
- visual/spatial;
- musical;
- interpersonal;
- intrapersonal;
- bodily/physical.

A detailed description of these can be found in the Nightingale Conant package, or in other published work by Howard Gardner (1993).

Stephen Covey has distilled many important attributes down in his *Seven Habits of Highly Effective People* (1986–95). With regard to accelerated learning three have a particular relevance.

1. Knowing how to make a clear vision of what success will be like.
2. Taking personal responsibility for own actions.
3. Creating the habit of reflecting and learning, then drawing lessons for the future.

It is also important not to restrict what can be achieved and to stretch comfort zones.

In addition to this process there are other key points to bear in mind when using accelerated learning techniques. These points are taken from Ostrander *et al*. (1994).

- The use of baroque music has been proven to aid the learning process. The slow sections normally run at 55–65 beats per minute and use sounds that produce natural high frequency harmonies. The effects this produces are:
  - a lowering of blood pressure;
  - steadying down of the heartbeat;
  - reduction in stress levels;
  - the beta waves in the brain decrease;
  - alpha brain waves (relaxation) increase;
  - the left and right sides of the brain become harmonized and synchronized;
  - a state of alert relaxation is created;
  - less energy is used, but to greater effect;
  - the brain becomes highly adaptive and aware.
- There is a wealth of statistical and medical evidence to support the view that a well-balanced, nutritious diet supports learning and in particular accelerated learning:
  - Lecithin, for example, has been proven to make people 25 per cent more effective. It also helps lower cholesterol and allows more oxygen to get to the brain.
  - The amino acid L-phenylalanine is found in meat, eggs, cheese and milk. This helps the process of memory and retention.
  - Glucose and glutamine provide brain energy.
  - Gingko improves memory, affecting concentration and can even restore short-term memory loss.
  - Zinc, magnesium and iron help in developing effective use of the brain.
  - Vitamins A, B complex and C assist with memory and abstract thinking.
  - Chlorophyll helps with keeping the mind and body free of disease.
- Using deep breathing techniques is very powerful in assisting the process of accelerated learning.

Autogenics is another useful way of self-development which can aid the process of accelerated learning. The process takes only 7–10 minutes per day but, if done for up to eight weeks, until it becomes a habit, will achieve great benefit. It has been described as psychological gymnastics or psychological fitness. Autogenics involves following specific steps in a verbatim way over a period of time and, apart from any learning benefit, reduces stress. (A good source of further information on autogenics is *Super Learning 2000*, by Sheila Ostrander *et al*.)

The role of NLP in accelerated learning is a vital one; but accelerated learning is not an NLP technique (or vice versa). Instead they are related fields that use the best that the other has to offer in order to become more effective themselves. Some trainers are now using accelerated learning techniques to learn NLP. The trainer who can teach themselves more, more quickly and effectively, and then help learners to achieve better results faster, is in a very strong position.

USING ACCELERATED LEARNING: EXERCISES

1. Use any of the relevant skills and techniques covered in this book. Most NLP techniques can be used to aid the process of accelerated learning. Choose ones that develop key strengths before moving on to new areas.
2. Apply NLP and accelerated learning techniques to a specific topic, eg learning a language, analyse what works, then move into other areas.

USING ACCELERATED LEARNING: KEY POINTS

☐   Have the building blocks in place.
  – Get learners motivated at the beginning.
  – Get information into right size chunks.
  – Put everything into a meaning and a context.
  – Help learners to create a positive self-image.
  – Create the right environment for learning.
  – Put information into all representation systems.
  – Make sure learners associate into the experience.
  – Get learners to go inside and use internal interactive visualization.
  – Avoid mindless repetition.
  – Use memory pegs.
  – Use mnemonics.
  – Use eye accessing cues.
  – Use your own and learners' sub-modalities.
☐   Follow the six step model.
  – Create a resourceful mind.
  – Use multi-sensory intake.
  – Explain using the seven intelligences.
  – Memorize the key events.
  – Show you know.
  – Reflect.

☐ Use other skills to aid the process:
   - big picture/little picture;
   - mind maps;
   - break into smaller chunks;
   - stay in up time;
   - ask lots of questions;
   - work with a partner(s);
   - develop own action checklists;
   - tick off, when completed;
   - read aloud;
   - put strong emphasis in your voice;
   - have a learning/training seat or posture;
   - use repeated, appropriate gestures to embed and create anchors;
   - use a highlighter;
   - move around/shift position;
   - use post-its, move them around;
   - visualize again, updating.
☐ Be aware of the seven intelligences:
   - linguistic;
   - mathematical/logical;
   - visual/spatial;
   - musical;
   - interpersonal;
   - intrapersonal;
   - bodily/physical.
☐ Be aware of other key points:
   - use of baroque music;
   - role of a balanced, nutritious diet;
   - use deep breathing techniques;
   - autogenics can aid the process.

USING ACCELERATED LEARNING: CASE STUDY

A colleague was trying to learn a foreign language by attending a night class. While finding this approach useful he was frustrated by its pace and was losing enthusiasm and motivation.

During a social conversation NLP was mentioned and the colleague became intrigued and curious as to how it might help him. We reviewed a number of possible strategies and he decided to work on maintaining a positive personal state, staying associated throughout the training, visualizing conversations internally and future pacing.

Over the next six months his rate of development astonished him (and the people in his class) and he has extended the principles into other areas of his working and personal life.

4.19 USING TIMELINES

Over the last few years timelines have become one of the most exciting and useful of the NLP techniques. Their prime use has been in individual therapy and counselling. But an insight into their background and use can aid the trainer, and they are being increasingly used in education and business circles.

The idea that supports timelines has been around for many thousands of years, in that people can sort and process time and memories into the past, present or future. So what has been discovered in the last ten years and what does it mean? Within the NLP field Richard Bandler made the early discoveries and these have been further developed by a number of people, in particular Tad James and Wyatt Woodsmall. Their book *Time Line Therapy and the Basis of Personality* (1988) is an essential read for anyone interested in the subject. In addition Tad James, who visits the UK at least once a year, carries out certified Time Line Therapies™, practitioner and master practitioner training, and is the leading edge trainer and developer in this field.

The first point to bear in mind is that the timeline is how the brain sorts and stores our memories. Most people at some level recognize that they must have a process for doing this, but have never really considered how or what it might mean. They accept that the brain must be able to make distinctions between past events, or past events and the here and now, but that is as far as they have taken it.

The other key issue to consider is what impact these memories, no matter how they are stored, have on people's personalities and how they respond to events.

Finding your timeline

There are two ways to do this:

- To find the general direction of the timeline:
  - Stop, go inside yourself and consider a past event and point toward the location where this memory is stored.
  - Stop, go inside yourself and consider an event you have coming up in the future, eg going on holiday, buying a car, moving house, changing your job. Point toward the location where this future event is stored.

    Normally the two locations pointed to will be in two different places. Relating this back to the Meta Program, regarding time, a conventional pattern would be:
  - *Through time* is often stored from left to right, or up and down, or in a 'V', or in some way that stores them *in front* of the person, not passing through their body.

- *In time* people, on the other hand, will have some of the memories stored behind them, or passing through part of their body or head.
- To find the timeline in more detail:
  (a) Remember something that happened one week ago, notice where it is stored.
  (b) Remember something that happened three months ago, notice where it is stored.
  (c) Remember something that happened six months ago, notice where it is stored.
  (d) Remember something that happened one year ago, notice where it is stored.
  (e) Remember something from five years ago, notice where it is stored.
  (f) Think of something that is going to happen in one week's time, notice where it is stored.
  (g) Repeat step 'f' for three months, six months, one year and five years ahead.

Note: It is vital to remember that although the word 'line' may imply something linear, timelines can be all sorts of shapes and sizes. I have known learners with corkscrew ones emerging from the top of their head, or a very short past one (even though the person was 47) and a future one that stretched out to the horizon, or one that did a 90-degree turn, or a circular one with breaks in it. It doesn't matter as long as it is right *for that person*. It is how they store time for themselves. There is also a danger that the person helping to elicit the timeline can influence the results by trying to make the respondent's timeline like their own, or fit a pattern they expect or have seen before.

One other factor is significant regarding timelines, and that is the use and power of language. English and other languages are rich with ways of describing and using time. The impact that this language has on how and why learners do, or don't do things should not be underestimated. The trainer can use matching words, phrases and representation of time sorts and then, by using shifting verb tenses, move to the future, embedding positive language to achieve a dramatic change for the learner.

The point about using these types of language is that, providing the trainer and learner are in rapport, the learner will have to make some change, at quite a deep level, in how they are thinking about, and responding to, the situation. For example the trainer who asked, 'What was your problem in learning this in the past?' could ask, 'What is your problem in learning this now?' moving the situation to *now*, where it can be tackled and sorted. Leaving it in the past will mean that the learner will not be able to find solutions for it.

Another example which is frequently used is using the suffix 'ing'. This is a very powerful language pattern and, in the context of timelines, an example would be 'what was the difficulty you were having in learning this topic?' compared with 'what was the learning difficulty you had?' Another future based use of the 'ing' suffix would be 'I am going to be tackling this topic'.

In therapy timelines are used for all sorts of topics, in particular:

- discovering the root cause of an issue;
- removing negative emotions;
- parts reframes;
- dealing with anxiety;
- dealing with limiting decisions;
- dealing with phobias;
- creating compelling futures.

In training, a knowledge and insight into timelines can help enormously. Listening to how learners describe and use time reveals a great deal about how they do what they do by being what they are.

One specific use of timelines for the trainer is for creating a compelling future. This process has been created by Tad James, who, as mentioned earlier, also runs seminars in the UK on this topic.

- State the goal so that it meets the SMART criteria, ie:
  - S Specific
  - M Measurable
  - A Attainable
  - R Realistic
  - T Timed.
- Get to the last step, ie what is the *last* thing that has to happen to know the goal has been achieved?
- Make a picture, or auditory representation, or kinesthetic representation.
- Step into the picture – associate.
- Adjust the qualities – using the sub-modalities.
- Step out of the picture – disassociate.
- Take the picture and float above now on the timeline.
- Energize the picture with four deep breaths – in through the nose, out through the mouth.
- Float out into the future.
- Insert the picture into the timeline at the 'last step' point.
- Notice the events between then and now and re-evaluate them to support the goal.
- Float back to now.
- Come back down to now.

This process is a very effective way to help learners achieve their goals and, used with other appropriate techniques, becomes part of the armoury of the trainer. Equally it can, of course, be used by trainers to help them achieve their own goals, whether in a training context or not.

Some trainers might wonder about where they can use timelines and this is a real issue. It can look a little mind blowing on first exposure. In my experience of using timelines in training, most people have been fascinated by them and willing to give them a try. It is important that no one feels coerced into using them, and if they want to sit out while we go through the phases that's fine. In some groups I would actually ask them to leave the room for a quick coffee break. In other situations it can be all right for them to stay. If they stay they often actually go through the process and comment favourably on it afterwards, particularly as they see that timelines can be used to develop key skills, such as coaching and appraising, as well as be applied in a wide variety of situations. One of the many factors that should not be underestimated regarding any of the NLP techniques is their capacity to intrigue and create curiosity.

It is also possible to use the notion of timelines to great effect, without actually going through the specific actions and steps. This requires using the idea of people processing the past, present and future in different ways to help 'unstick' them or to help give them a direction.

USING TIMELINES: CASE STUDY

One example was in a meeting to design a new training programme that would consist of eight courses over a three year period. As the meeting developed everyone became bogged down in the detail and the here and now, resulting in frustration and bickering. The question that achieved the breakthrough was: 'Let's all put ourselves three years down the line looking back at the training after it has been completed successfully. What will have been the key factors that made the training achieve its objectives?' This question changed the whole tenor of the meeting and allowed it to be completed successfully. It also doesn't require any specific knowledge of timelines, just the notion of how they work.

The other interesting point is how many people notice this sort of intervention. Most people do not recognize how something was done, but do pick up on, and respond positively to, the fact that a breakthrough has been made, a different dynamic created, or an objective achieved.

USING TIMELINES: EXERCISES

1. Use the timeline elicitation exercises covered in this section.
2. Combine timelines with other relevant skills and techniques, eg sub-modalities, being aware of invisibles.
3. Use timelines as part of preparation for your own trainings.

USING TIMELINES: KEY POINTS

☐ Learners sort time into past, present and future.
☐ Follow the 'finding the timeline' process.
☐ Learners normally store either in 'through' or 'in' time.
☐ Follow the detailed timeline process.
☐ The 'line' may not be linear.
☐ Be aware of the impact of language in sorting and using time.
☐ Use matching words, phrases, representations, shifting verb tenses, positive language to achieve dramatic change.
☐ Use the 'ing' suffix to achieve change.
☐ Use timelines to create intrigue and curiosity.

4.20 USING FUTURE PACING

Future pacing is a classic NLP technique in that it gives a shape, structure and sequence to a process that many people, particularly in sport and business, already use because they know it works. This is especially so if it is repeated on a regular basis, which creates the opportunity to anchor the behaviour as well.

The process is based upon identifying a situation or context where a particular behaviour or outcome is required, and creating a mental process which allows for successful achievement of that outcome. This helps tee up successful completion of the outcome in the situation where it is required.

Like many NLP skills, future pacing can be used along with other techniques or added on to the end of them to help establish the appropriate mental processes. It is also a generative exercise which, used regularly, will become habitual and can be used in every type of situation that people face. This technique is one of the simplest yet most powerful in the whole field of NLP.

USING FUTURE PACING: EXERCISES

1. This exercise can be done at the end of a training:
    - Choose something learnt on the course.
    - Anchor the learned behaviour using VAKOG.
    - Think of a time in the future when using this behaviour or learning would be of benefit: choose a specific situation.
    - Choose how you would know when to use the behaviour or learning, ie decide on a signal. .
    - Run a movie of the future event (with sounds and feelings).
    - Fire the anchor; with the anchor fired carry on running the movie.
    - Repeat four or five times.
2. Add future pacing on to the end of any appropriate NLP technique.
3. Use future pacing in all aspects of life.

USING FUTURE PACING: KEY POINTS

☐ It is already used by many sports and business people.
☐ It helps create the mental processes for successful use of a behaviour or achievement of an outcome.
☐ It can be combined with other NLP techniques.
☐ It is a generative process.
☐ Used regularly it will become habitual.

USING FUTURE PACING: CASE STUDY

Someone on a training course was very hesitant about how her boss would respond to her after the course had finished. Their relationship was fraught, not very open and uncomfortable.

In reviewing the course the delegate decided that one of the specific areas she wished to tackle was this relationship, in order to receive better feedback on job performance in the future.

An outcome was agreed and the delegate worked through the future pacing process five or six times, before leaving the course, and then again before seeing her boss.

The meeting with the boss, while not going completely the way the delegate wanted, went better than she originally thought it would. It has provided the foundation for improving both the quality of the feedback and the relationship itself.

4.21 USING META PROGRAMS

Over the last 20 years NLP has contributed an enormous amount to the field of human development and interactions. Within this context one of the most valuable assets it has given us is Meta Programs. For the trainer these are absolutely essential tools.

The basis of Meta Programs is that the brain, because it has such vast potential and so much information to process, has to put some sort of sense or shape into how it does this. These senses or shapes allow people to make sense of all the information that comes at them and also determines the value put on the information and the response to it. They are the key drivers for the behaviour people then do, making sense and meaning to them and explaining the actions carried out. This means taking information, however received, and, by filtering and sorting it, being able to create and sustain their view about the world and how it affects them.

The original work on Meta Programs was carried out by Cameron-Bandler in the early 1980s. This early work has been further developed by many people within the NLP community, and is continuing all the time.

The real beginning of Meta Programs starts with Carl Jung and his work on psychological types, which provided the foundation. This was followed up by the development of the Myers Briggs profile. Leslie Cameron-Bandler also based her original ideas on work carried out by Noam Chomsky in 1957. In his work Chomsky pointed out that people use three filters to make sense of the world. This is because the conscious mind can only pay attention to a limited amount of information. According to George Miller, an American psychologist, this is 7 ± 2. Therefore the mind has to decide which, out of all the information available, is the best to pay attention to. It does this by a combination of three processes; deletion, distortion and generalization. These also form the patterns for the basic Meta Model violations covered earlier in this book.

Deletion
This is the process of deciding what to ignore. In training, it may be new facts that challenge a long-held view.

Distortion
People will distort things in order to make sense of them or be able to make sense of them based upon views already held. In training, this can be twisting something new to sustain long-held views.

Generalization
This is where people take a small number of examples and then create a rule that applies to all situations. People need rules to make sense of the world and will feel challenged and threatened if new information does not fit. In training this can be looking for the one skill, technique, strategy or initiative that could be applied to all situations.

Note: When talking about information in the context of Meta Programs, it is important to remember that everything received via the senses, ie pictures, words, feelings and sensations, smell and taste, are information. We are not just considering facts, numbers, etc, everything around us is information. This means that people (including trainers and learners) have normal patterns of behavioural response and they take their experience and then create their behaviour. Even the most unlikely subjective experience will be sorted or altered to put a sense or shape to it. These patterns are their Meta Programs.

Where this becomes useful to the trainer is that it means one can organize how to put things across so that they will be received more positively by the learner. This will be based on observing how the learners communicate (at all levels) and then matching and pacing them to help them learn more effectively. In addition should there be any conflict or problems between the trainer and the learners, it will be the Meta Programs that reveal where these differences lie.

All of the work carried out regarding Meta Programs indicates that there are patterns of behaviour which can be observed and often predicted. This obviously does not mean that all people are totally predictable 100 per cent of the time. The glory of dealing with human beings is their infinite capacity to surprise, and NLP has given us many more ways to be surprised. Every time the trainer believes he has recognized a pattern in behaviour in a learner, they may well respond differently. This for all of us is good news *but* the predominant patterns will still be evident and applied in certain specific situations or contexts.

This issue of context or situation is a very important one for the trainer to bear in mind. People in general will behave in different ways at different times *dependent on the context or situation*. For example, the classic contrast could be home and work, or it could be with a partner or with friends, or playing sport and going to church. The Meta Programs, therefore, may well be specific to the context or situation.

Many people may have had mixed experiences of previous training and therefore their Meta Programs related to attending a training course may be different to any of the other patterns they may use. This explains the occasional negative, or even hostile, response that many trainers have to deal with. It also gives them the opportunity to be able to respond in a different, more effective way.

Moving toward or moving away

This Meta Program is based on why something is important to the learner, ie the values that apply. It is based on whether something is attractive, rewarding and pleasurable, or should be avoided due to some potential failure or punishment.

Moving toward

Overview: Learners who want to be at the training. They ask questions, jump into leading syndicates, and don't always recognize that other people are not always following.

How to spot them:

- Speak from an 'I' position.
- Are clear about what they want from the training.
- Will include other learners in.
- Will get lots of reading.
- Will not want to sit still for too long.
- Will use phrases like 'let's do it', 'let's go for it', let's get on with it'.
- Will talk about achievements, benefits, etc.

How to help them:

- Work on their objectives and plans.
- Show how what you are doing will help.
- Show how the training will help.
- Use incentives not threats.
- Remove blocks from their way.

Moving away

Overview: Learners who wait for others to ask or do things (unless they can ask a really difficult question). May want to over-analyse information rather than do something with it. They tend not to want to do syndicate exercises (unless it means being able to move away from the trainer).

How to spot them:

- Will talk about learning as if it just happens to them.
- Will use lots of words about problems, things to be avoided.
- Will not complete sentences properly.
- Will use lots of passive language.
- Will want to understand all the theories.
- Will look for the contra example.
- Will be clear about what they don't want or can't use from the training.
- Will sit relatively still and passive for long periods.

How to help them:

- Use words and phrases like solve, prevent, there won't be any problems.
- Be clear about what they do and don't want from the training.

- Look ahead for any potential problem areas.
- Show them you understand and can, and will, still help.
- Help them to clarify their objectives.

Note: In this book we are using the two extremes in each Meta Program pattern. It is important to remember that for each pattern there is also the middle ground. Therefore, the complete pattern for moving toward and moving away is:

- moving toward;
- moving toward with moving away;
- equally toward and away;
- moving away with moving toward;
- moving away.

This factor will apply to all the other Meta Program patterns.

Possibility/Necessity

This Meta Program is based on the amount of choices that people make. What reason do they have for their actions?

Possibility
Overview: Learners who are possibility focused are enthusiastic, keen to try new things, look out for new situations and challenges and will often change something even if it is working well.
How to spot them:

- Will tell the trainer what they want to do.
- Will ask opportunity type questions.
- Will believe they have control for themselves.
- Interested in new choices and options.
- Will see potential in new material.
- Will use words like hope, wish, want, possibility, can do.
- Will talk about doing things.
- Will have a strong future focus.

How to help them:

- Help them to look at new material/insights.
- Help them to see the opportunity for growth and/or change.
- Help them to see how they can use what is being learnt.
- Don't tie them down to following a rigid set of instructions.
- Use words like new, different, choice, options, possibilities, alternatives.

Necessity

Overview: Learners who are attending because there is no choice. They are not looking to get anything out of the training except survival or damage limitation. They prefer traditional ways of learning and sticking with what is known and safe.

How to spot them:

- Will be closed in their non-verbal communication.
- Will sit back and wait for things to happen.
- May 'go through the motions'.
- Will want to over-analyse everything.
- Will clam up about, or overly question new topics or information.
- Will use words like must, need, have to.
- Will give evidence of not being in control of life.
- Will not like too many new options.

How to help them:

- Show respect for input they know.
- Show respect for their views.
- Fully explain anything new.
- Be structured and systematic in explaining exercises.
- Be specific regarding outcomes of learning.
- Use words like proven, known, correct, right way.

USING META PROGRAMS: CASE STUDY

During an outdoor training course a participant was unwilling to try some of the activities. In discussing this issue he used lots of moving away from and necessity language, for example, 'I suppose I must do this but I don't really see the point'.

Rather than try to persuade him, the trainer asked questions, matched the Meta Programs, helped him find what could come out of it, explained the thinking behind the activities, and showed where it had worked previously.

The participant suggested trying one or two of the activities, found them to be OK and joined in the rest of the course. Afterwards it transpired that he had hated sport at school, but had been forced to participate.

Self/Other

This Meta Program is based on whether the learner naturally notices the behaviour of other learners or is only aware of themselves.

Self

Overview: Very self-absorbed, give great attention to their own feelings and thoughts. Can often seem preoccupied and oblivious to other learners on the course.

How to spot them:

- Tend not to show emotions.
- Only pick up on what is said, rather than how it is said.
- Sit back and reflect.
- Don't spot what is happening around them.
- Not overly skilled in interpersonal communication.
- Will not reveal much in their face.

How to help them:

- Keep the input focused on specifics.
- Show them you understand them.
- Don't try too hard to build a relationship with them.
- Be very clear about what is said.
- Do not get too drawn into them.
- Do not show evidence of having taken their response in a personal way.

Others

Overview: They respond to other people on the course and are expressive with, and perceptive of, other learners. They pick up with others very quickly and get along well with other people. They will often help others to find solutions and may over communicate.

How to spot them:

- Will respond to how something is said as well as what is said.
- Will nod a lot in agreement.
- Will be fairly animated.
- Will be aware of how others are responding and feeling.
- Will look around the room to observe others.
- Will often be the group spokesperson.

How to help them:

- Be expressive in communicating.
- Show enthusiasm for the group.
- Circulate and mix.
- Ensure all of group understand before moving on.
- Mix over breaks and meals.

- Show rapport, empathy and respect for the group.
- Show how materials can be used with others.
- Talk about how others have used materials.

Similarity/Difference

This Meta Program is based on how learners respond to change and how often change occurs.

Similarity
Overview: These learners tend not to like change and find it hard to adapt to new information, skills, techniques. In the end they may accept change but will initiate change even less often. They will delete lots of different types of information in order to find the similarity. They tend to stay in the same job or company for a long time.

How to spot them:

- Will look for how materials are being taught and relate to previous learnings.
- Will look for common themes.
- Will use words like similar, same, common, like.
- Will test their views for matches with other people on the course.
- Will point out how things haven't changed.
- Will be conservative with new ideas.

How to help them:

- Show them similarities in the new materials with the old.
- Show how new skills and techniques build on past.
- Show areas of commonality.
- Show that you are both working to the same goals.
- Build upon what they already know.

Difference
Overview: These learners love change and like the idea that what is being taught is new and different. It is an attraction that no one else in the organization may know about it. They change jobs or organizations frequently and need a constant spur and stimulus.

How to spot them:

- Will look for what is different in materials.
- Will be anti the 'status quo'.
- Will look for what isn't being covered in the training.
- Will want to stand out by being anti-system, the company, or whatever else is happening.
- Will look towards the next steps, not the current ones.

How to help them:

- Show them how materials are new.
- Show them how skills and techniques will change things.
- Show them how they will be different by having attended the training.
- Use words like new, different, unique, only, unheard of.
- Train by mismatching, eg say to them 'I don't know if you could use this'; they will respond by saying they can.
- Use your own personal experiences to show how new everything is.

Chunk size – General/Specific

This Meta Program relates to how learners prefer to take in information, whether they like the big picture with the overall view, or whether they need the detail in order to make sense and shape of things. Learners will normally be able to move from one to the other; recognizing which way this works for them is very useful.

This also forms a core part of the big picture/little picture technique covered in 2.10 (page 54).

General
Overview: Learners who prefer to chunk by generalities will look for the big picture. They like ideas and concepts. See everything all at the same time rather than in small steps. Express a lack of interest in too many details and may become bored fairly easily. They may not like, or be good at, following through on specific actions.

How to spot them:

- Will ask for the overview or big picture.
- Will ask for and discuss concepts and ideas.
- Will leap from idea to idea without following them through systematically.
- Will use sentences with few details.
- They will give evidence of becoming bored with details and may actually ask the trainer to move on.

How to help them:

- Show them the big picture and general overview first.
- Don't go into too much detail too soon.
- Watch for them becoming bored.
- Use a range of training techniques/materials.
- Use words like idea, concept, framework, generally.

- Be prepared for them to make big leaps with ideas quickly and respond accordingly.

Specifics

Overview: These learners prefer information and materials to be broken down into specific, obvious steps. They will only form conclusions if all the data is available. Need to have clear instructions and lots of real, solid examples. They can sometimes have a real difficulty in prioritizing what to use from a training course.

How to spot them:

- Will talk in, and ask for, details.
- If they lose their way with a question they will start all over again, or continue from where they got to.
- Only see the 'here and now', rather than the end product.
- Will use lots of adjectives and adverbs.

How to help them:

- Show them, in a step-by-step way, how materials can be used.
- Don't generalize too much with them.
- Use words like details, sequences, precisely, exactly, specifically, first, second, third, schedule, plan.
- Get them to relate back to you, in their own way, what they have learnt.
- Get them to draw up a plan for implementing learnings.

Frame of reference – Internal/External

This Meta Program relates to how learners judge the response to their own actions. Do they check outside or inside themselves? It's about where the final judgement and evaluation is made, and where they feel the real responsibility lies. It is also about the source for motivation and values regarding self.

This Meta Program can sometimes be confused with self/others. The distinction is that this program is about where the judgement regarding responsibility is made.

Internal

Overview: Learners using this pattern go inside for their emotions and will check with themselves as to whether the course is going well. This means that they won't always accept negative comments if they feel that they felt good about something themselves, and will query the opinion of the person making the comments.

They will gather information then decide upon it for themselves.

Because the ultimate check is internal they see directives as information and treat them accordingly. In addition they are very clear about their own standards, beliefs and values.

How to spot them:

- Will tell you what they believe/know.
- Will not want others to decide on the use or validity of training.
- Will not give feedback to others on the training.
- Will use words like 'I know', 'it feels right'.
- Will not reveal very much through their facial expressions or gestures.
- Will talk from the inside out in responding.
- Will pause to reflect on own outside view.

How to help them:

- Show them how material fits in with their standards, values and beliefs.
- Show them you respect their point of view.
- Show them that you are not forcing them, it's OK for them to decide.
- Use phrases like 'try it out and decide for yourself', 'here's some material so you can decide'.
- Help them to clarify their own thinking.

External

Overview: These learners require feedback and input from other people and outside sources. They tend to take their standards, beliefs and values from others, or be heavily influenced by them. Their view of the world and motivation comes from the people around them and they will decide how well a training is doing by how others are responding to it.

How to spot them:

- Will look for comparisons with other people to form a view.
- Will check out their views and ideas with others on the course.
- Will watch the trainer and others, watching for a response to check that something is all right.
- Will often react to information as if it was an order.
- Will use words like 'they say', or 'everybody knows'.
- Will tend to look for approval.
- Will require a lot of praise and support.

How to help them:

- Show them what other people think and do.
- Give them lots of praise and feedback.

- Get them to check the information out with others.
- Check who they are using as the authority, then build on it.
- Use phrases like 'the others have noticed that...', 'the experts say that...', 'a well-known point of view is...', 'it's generally accepted by people that...'.

Where people place their interest

This is a slightly different Meta Program in that it covers a range of topics and indicates the priorities the learner will place on a particular situation in order to give it importance and be able to retrieve their memories.

The classic categories are:

- activity;
- information;
- people;
- place;
- things;
- time.

One way of establishing what order these operate in, for a particular situation or context, is to ask questions. For example, 'Why did you choose that holiday?' will reveal a lot of useful information. Other examples, such as 'What is your favourite hobby and why?' will also reveal their particular priorities. In training, questions regarding favourite topics, real-life experiences, issues encountered, can be equally helpful.

Activity
Learners with this as a primary driver will talk about what they did, or what can be done with materials. They will focus on what is actually going on; they can become bored very quickly and want to get into action.

Information
Learners who have this focus want to know and have access to all the information available. They are interested in ideas and will often want to give the trainer information, or swap information with them. Some might also be specific about the type of information they are interested in, eg activities, place, people, things or time.

People
This focus is based on who is part of any process or activity. In discussing a previous course they will talk about the people first, who said or did what, the impact that was created. They will be seen frequently talking to other people on the course.

Place
These learners need to feel comfortable with the environment and location for the training. They also have a strong sense of where they are coming

from. They may feel uncomfortable with having to move seats during a training and will put their materials into set places.

Things

Learners with this as a primary driver place great importance on having the right tools or possessions. These could include car, house, equipment, office computer. It is worthwhile to check out what importance they attach to people; if very little they may isolate themselves a little from the rest of the course.

Time

Great attention is placed on 'when' something happened and in what sequence. They will be very specific about dates and what occurred. They will check the timetable and want the times to be adhered to. In syndicate sessions they will try to keep things on schedule.

Other aspects of Meta Programs which can be useful for the trainer include the following.

Convincer pattern

Learners will each have their own way to become convinced about what is being learnt. The trainer should be aware of how these processes work.

Automatic

These learners will base their judgements on small amounts of materials or input. They will leap to an end conclusion without being bothered about having to wait and will often find it hard to change their minds about their decisions.

Consistent

This can be a slow, demanding process for a trainer as these learners need to consistently re-evaluate material before deciding upon it and then they will need to re-evaluate again. They will often go back to a point which appeared to have been accepted by everybody and start discussing it all over again.

Number of examples

The process that these learners go through requires them to have materials gone through a number of times before they decide to accept them. They will want to have instructions for tasks repeated and then may well check them through again with others.

Period of time

Being rushed or forced to accept things too quickly makes these learners uncomfortable. New ideas or information in particular need to be allowed to 'seep' through before a decision is made to accept and be convinced.

Time

This Meta Program is about how learners store and use time. Some learners will have a focus on previous experiences and learning, some on the 'here and now', their current experience. Others will have a 'this is how I am going to use this' direction. A number may not have any particular time awareness (atemporal).

In addition, some learners may use past experience as a reason or block for not being able to go forward, eg 'I've never been confident making presentations and never will be'. This indicates a belief that the future is pre-set (at least as far as they are concerned). Equally others might say 'I've handled things in the past, I'm sure I'll be OK in the future'.

How learners process time

1. past – looking backwards;
2. present – here and now;
3. future – how I am going to use this;
4. atemporal – not aware of time.

In addition to these four patterns learners will tend to store time in one of two ways.

Through time
Learners who store using through time tend to:

- be very aware of how long things take;
- be on time (and expect others to be);
- see events as being connected with each other;
- go through a long process before arriving at a decision;
- want more time on topics than the trainer has given;
- have difficulty remembering one specific instance.

In time
Learners who store using in time tend to:

- be very aware of the here and now;
- get caught up in events as they occur;
- be late for appointments;
- make quicker decisions;
- prefer the beginning of subjects/exercises on training courses;
- access memories as one specific event.

These distinctions can be very useful for the trainer to be aware of and utilize to achieve maximum benefit for the learner. The section on timelines (see 4.19, page 162) goes into this area in more detail.

Current developments in Meta Programs

As with everything in NLP, Meta Programs are being continually revised and updated, nothing is new or current for very long.

The Meta Programs used in this book are the 'standard' model, which have been used, validated and accepted for some time. Those trainers interested in further reading on this topic should read *Time Line Therapy and the Basis of Personality* by Tad James and Wyatt Woodsmall (1988) and *Words that Change Minds* by Shelle Rose Charvet (1996).

Uses for Meta Programs

At the beginning of this section I said that Meta Programs were an invaluable tool for the trainer. Having worked through them, particularly for the first time, they can look a little intimidating, something else for the trainer to think or worry about; plus, of course, one has to consider how the Meta Programs relate to each other.

Because Meta Programs explain why learners do what they do, particularly if what they do is different to what the trainer wants or believes they should do, they give the trainer the opportunity to 'second position' an individual or the group to achieve maximum benefit.

Applications in organizations are:

- training and development;
- team building;
- interviewing;
- appraising;
- coaching;
- negotiating;
- selling;
- marketing;
- counselling;
- career planning;
- change management;
- working on corporate culture issues.

Within the specific area of training, the trainer can respond by:

- recognizing why some things work for some learners but not for others;
- altering an approach that isn't working;
- doing more of what is working;
- removing learning blocks for individuals;
- using appropriate language in sessions;
- 'fine-tuning' individuals to help them;

- learning about their own style and its effectiveness;
- developing greater personal flexibility;
- matching materials and inputs to certain audiences, eg scientists, designers, manufacturers;
- building on the motivation of groups/individuals;
- creating their own materials;
- understanding why someone is finding something particularly difficult;
- making training even more fun and effective for all concerned.

USING META PROGRAMS: EXERCISES

1. Apply the various Meta Programs to yourself, in a variety of different contexts, including various aspects of training.
2. Listen to learners' language to get clues as to their Meta Program. Ask effective questions to substantiate evidence covered in this section.
3. Use the SWISH exercise (see page 192).
4. Combine with any other relevant NLP skills and techniques, eg language patterns, creating new learning patterns, switching roles and styles, being aware of invisibles.
5. Ask questions that will help elicit the sub-modalities of Meta Programs (without having to mention sub-modalities at all) eg when you think of that (learning) experience, how do you see it? How does it sound? How does it make you feel?

USING META PROGRAMS: KEY POINTS

☐ Learners will use Meta Programs to make sense of the training.
☐ Meta Programs are based on the patterns of:
  – deletion;
  – distortion;
  – generalization.
☐ Information is received in all five senses.
☐ Trainers can respond more flexibly and appropriately.
☐ Learners will always have the capacity to surprise.
☐ People may respond differently in different contexts or situations.
☐ The key Meta Programs are:
  – moving toward/away;
  – possibility/necessity;
  – self/other;
  – similarity/difference;
  – chunk size – general/specific;
  – internal/external – frame of reference;
  – where people place their interest; ie: activity, information, people, place, things and time.

- ☐ Additional Meta Programs to consider are convincer patterns:
  - – automatic;
  - – consistent;
  - – number of examples;
  - – period of time.
- ☐ Use Meta Programs for:
  - – training and development;
  - – team building;
  - – interviewing;
  - – appraising;
  - – coaching;
  - – negotiating;
  - – selling;
  - – marketing;
  - – counselling;
  - – career planning;
  - – change management;
  - – working on corporate culture issues.
- ☐ Within training, specific uses are:
  - – recognizing why things do or don't work for learners;
  - – altering an approach that isn't working;
  - – doing more of what is working;
  - – removing learning blocks for individuals;
  - – using appropriate language in sessions;
  - – fine-tuning individuals to help them;
  - – learning about own style and effectiveness;
  - – developing greater personal flexibility;
  - – matching materials and inputs to certain audiences, eg scientists, designers, manufacturers;
  - – building on the motivation of groups/individuals;
  - – creating own materials;
  - – understanding why someone is finding something particularly difficult;
  - – making training even more fun and effective for all concerned.

USING META PROGRAMS: CASE STUDY

During a training course on negotiation skills one HR manager, who did a great deal of negotiating, stated his view that negotiations were a matter of right and wrong, and winning and losing.

Part of the course included a brief session on Meta Programs, and when that point was reached he was asked to explore his *in the negotiations context*.

Having done this he was asked to think about the Meta Programs of the person he most frequently dealt with, not from the point of view of the trade union, but as an individual.

The manager was amazed at how many similarities there were, but also recognized that there were key differences, and that it was these differences that always provided the stumbling block. He realized that, when he came up against these differences, his strategy had been to push harder and create even more of a blockage and breakdown.

The other key issue he recognized was that it was possible far more than he had imagined to 'win-win' and that he had been contributing to a number of the problem areas.

Feedback later indicated a better relationship for both parties.

4.22 TASKING PEOPLE

This process assists the trainer in helping individuals or groups. It normally operates outside the formal training, although individuals might have tasks to complete within a training session, eg using a specific skill in a syndicate exercise.

Tasks are normally based on doing more of something, although on occasions if someone is, for example, dominating a group the task might be to do less of something, or do something completely different. Tasks, therefore, are used to stretch and challenge learners. They would normally be private between the trainer and the learner, although in some circumstances it is appropriate to make them public.

The feedback loop should always be completed by the learner going back to the trainer about how they did the task, what happened and how they will use it in future. The trainer can then, if appropriate, help the learner agree an outcome, set an anchor, future pace or any other NLP (or other) technique that will help.

Some examples of tasks:

- leading a syndicate exercise;
- chairing a group review;
- speaking to everyone on the course over lunch;
- sitting back until four other people have contributed;
- making a presentation;
- giving feedback to someone else on the course.

TASKING PEOPLE: EXERCISES

1. Give learners specific tasks.
2. Combine with other relevant NLP techniques, eg creating rapport, using language patterns, using Meta Programs.
3. Use different tasks for different learners.

TASKING PEOPLE: KEY POINTS

☐ Normally agreed outside formal training.
☐ Carried out at any point either formal or informal during the programme.
☐ Based on doing more of something, less of something, or something completely different.
☐ The feedback loop back to the trainer should be completely based on:
  – how they did it;
  – what happened;
  – how they will use it in future.
☐ The process can then be concluded by agreeing an outcome, setting an anchor, future pacing, or any other appropriate NLP (or other) technique.

TASKING PEOPLE: CASE STUDY

Someone on a people skills course, who wanted some assistance to make a greater impact, was tasked to match and pace people before leaping in to speak. They did this consistently over the two and a half day programme and received positive comments on it during the group feedback session at the end.

4.23 USING CHUNKING

Chunking has already been covered in 4.21 Using Meta Programs (page 167), so a quick revisit is all that is required here.

Learners will have a preference for chunking information, facts, materials, etc into either general chunks, ie big picture generalities, or specific chunks, ie detailed, small steps. They will give evidence of their preferences by the questions they ask and the amount of attention they pay to various parts of the training.

These preferences will be a major factor regarding their response to any training and 'mismatching' can render some, or all, of the training ineffective.

USING CHUNKING: EXERCISES

1. Give information in different size chunks at different points in the training.
2. Fine-tune to individual learner's chunk size preferences.
3. Combine with other NLP skills and techniques, eg creating rapport, unsticking people, changing learner states.
4. Practise and become aware of own chunk size preferences specific to situations and contexts.

USING CHUNKING: KEY POINTS

☐ Learners will have a preference for general or specific chunks in training.
☐ Large chunk is big picture, generalities.
☐ Small chunk is details, step by step.
☐ Mismatching can adversely affect the training.
☐ Read 4.21 Using Meta Programs – chunk size, general or specific (page 167), for more detail on this topic.

4.24 USING SUB-MODALITIES

Sub-modalities are one of those parts of NLP that often create confusion and wonderment in equal measures in those who come across them for the first time.

Put simply sub-modalities are the 'language of the brain' ie how the brain sorts and processes information and, like all other individual aspects of how we do things, everyone uses sub-modalities differently. This applies to learning as much as to everything else.

The key points regarding sub-modalities are that the brain has its own way of storing and using information and the way it does this is by using sub-modalities. For example if someone is asked to describe a happy experience in sub-modality language they are likely to describe it in a different way to a sad experience.

Normally this would mean that the happy experience was brighter, probably closer, larger, louder, at a different speed, felt different inside, whereas the bad experience could be dimmer and greyer, slower, felt in a different place, further away, etc. Even quite similar experiences can be stored with slight differences and these differences can mean quite varying but important things.

The classic sub-modality divisions are:

Visual

- Associated/disassociated – ie seen through our own eyes (associated) or seen from elsewhere (disassociated).
- Location – where is the learner looking when reliving the experience.
- Distance – how far away is the image?
- Colour – is the image in full colour through to black and white?
- Size – how large or small is the image?
- Brightness – is the image normal, brighter, or duller than normal?
- Movement – is the image like a movie or a slide show?
- Speed – are the movements faster or slower than normal?

- Clarity – is the image clear and focused or blurred?
- Duration – how long does the image last?
- Depth – is the image two or three dimensional?
- Frame/panorama – what is the lens angle?

Auditory

- Volume – is the sound loud or soft?
- Location – where is the sound coming from?
- Distance – how far away is the sound?
- Tone – is the sound soft/hard or low/high?
- Words/sounds – are there either or both?
- Stereo – is it mono through to stereo?
- Whose voice – is it own voice/other or both?
- Speed – is the sound slower or faster than normal?
- Duration – how long does the sound last?
- Continuous – is the sound interrupted or continuous?
- Clarity – is the sound dull or clear?
- Associated/disassociated – as per 'visual'.

Kinesthetic

This is to include both tactile sensations as well as internal feelings, emotions, muscles.

- Location – where is the place, where is it felt?
- Shape – what shape is the feeling?
- Size – how small or large is the feeling?
- Temperature – is the feeling cold through to hot?
- Pressure – is the feeling soft through to hard?
- Duration – how long does the feeling last?
- Frequency – how often is the feeling felt?
- Movement – does the feeling move location at any point?
- Intensity – is the feeling weak through to strong?
- Texture – is the feeling smooth through to rough?

We have focused on the VAK aspects of sub-modalities since, in western societies in particular, these three are the prime ones that are used and can be easily established. But the olfactory and gustatory categories should not be ignored. If they are mentioned they are likely to be extremely important and should be noted.

The best way to learn about sub-modalities is to 'play' with them, either by oneself or, preferably, with a colleague. It is important to bear in mind when one is asking or answering the questions that it is not just the extremes that should be sought; any shade of difference is interesting and of potential use to the person reliving the experience.

The second point is that when getting inside the experience it is important to access the state as close to how it was *at the time, then* to go through the sub-modalities. If this is not done the quality and worth of the output will be less useful.

Therefore it's best to choose experiences that are not too far away from each other, eg:

- happy – Normal – sad
- like – Normal – don't like
- positive – Normal – negative

rather than two issues which are miles away from each other, where the differences would be obvious.

The basic steps for establishing sub-modalities are:

1. Choose a positive training experience.
2. Relive (access) the experience (state).
3. Work through the sub-modalities and checklist (preferably with someone else asking the questions) staying *in the experience*, don't search for anything, just let whatever is there come out. *Note* it is important that the person asking the questions doesn't judge, analyse or try to influence the output. They should take verbatim notes of answers and comments made. These notes should be based *only* on the process, the content should not be gone into. Therefore, the questioner never needs to know the actual experience. If they are told, the danger is in re-living the experience, analysing it and putting their own judgement on it. For this process it is only how the experience is stored that is relevant.
4. Choose a negative training experience (but borderline negative).
5. As step 2.
6. As step 3.
7. Questioner gives feedback based on sub-modalities noted.
8. Discussion on output, in particular looking at key sub-modality differences.

This very simple process can really make a lot of difference to people of all types, particularly learners. It has never occurred to most people that they store their experiences in different ways, although most people are aware that some things feel better than others and that some images are brighter or greyer than others.

USING SUB-MODALITIES: CASE STUDIES

Two experiences which happened during a training course illustrate this point.

On one course, while getting learners to analyse their previous learning experiences and the impact these had had on their subsequent response to training, we ran the exercise based on a positive and negative experience. To the amazement of one of the participants they found that they were associated (ie living it from the inside out, seeing it through their own eyes) in the case of the negative experience, while in the positive one they were disassociated, seeing it as if from the outside (as on a screen). This meant that the negative experience was the more deeply felt and had anchored them into a bad state regarding their ability to learn.

The second example concerns an accountant attending a training course. The rationale for the course was based on a combination of 360 degree profiling and management competencies.

The company had its own competency language based on a set of 19 competencies. Prior to attending the course participants were, with guaranteed anonymity, profiled by their immediate manager, two peer colleagues and three subordinates. They then arrived on the programme with their own set profile and the average other, 360 degree profile.

The purpose of the three day course was to give participants a menu of choices, skills and techniques which they could then apply to the competencies they had chosen to develop. Six months after the original three days they would reconvene for a further two days, having been profiled for a second time, to review the results.

As part of the original three day programme a short exercise on sub-modalities was included to give participants more insight into how they did things in particular relation to the competencies, ie with a competency they were strong on did they store and respond to it in a different way to a weak competency?

The process was demonstrated by the two trainers to the usual intrigue and scepticism, particularly from the accountant. Participants were then split into pairs to go through the experience for themselves. Fifteen minutes later the response was completely different. He felt that all his learning blocks had been explained and clarified and he was hungry to go to the next stage, which is, having got the sub-modality differences, how can they be used to purposeful effect?

Examples of how to use sub-modalities in this way are shown below. The first is based upon apathy about something to being motivated about something, a situation most learners find themselves in. This exercise is once again designed for two people, although like most NLP based exercises there are distinct advantages in having an observer to give feedback on the process to both parties.

Action steps

1. Create rapport (this should be done at beginning in all exercises).
2. Choose the situations.

3. Ask ecology question, ie are they happy to work on topics, is it OK to change?
4. Access motivated state.
5. Elicit sub-modalities for motivated state (only process based *not* content).
6. Break state.
7. Access apathy state.
8. Elicit sub-modalities for apathetic state.
9. Break state.
10. Take a couple of the important differences. (If the person asking the questions is not sure they should ask the person reliving the experiences.) These are called either key drivers or critical sub-modalities.
11. The person reliving the experiences should then take the two or three critical differences and move them from the motivated into the apathetic state. This is normally straightforward. Person B should watch for signs of change in A, eg physiology, eye accessing, language.

    Note: It is important that if there is a B, the person assisting the process, that:
    – They future pace at the end and don't leave A in an apathetic state.
    – B tells A to take, and map, the critical sub-modalities areas.
    – B is congruent to A when eliciting the sub-modalities.
    – B stays focused on A and doesn't get into analysing or considering their own experiences.
    – B uses appropriate and matching language to help A elicit sub-modalities.
12. This process can then be followed by a future pace to help A the next time they need to use the skills and, if appropriate, an anchor. Their response to the previous apathetic state should now be completely different, ie motivated, and should be obvious to others.

Note: Like most NLP techniques this is a generative process, ie the more it is done the more natural and embedded it becomes. The key point is that the person A can actually do this for themselves whenever they require it. Once they know and understand the process they can turn it on at will; it is possible to put all experiences through the sub-modality process.

Another famous version of this sub-modality change process is known as 'wishing to wanting'.

The same steps are followed as for the apathy to motivation process but this time substitute wishing for apathy and wanting for motivated. The purpose of this process is that, for most people, things they wish for are more distant and unattainable compared with things they actually *want*. Going through these steps helps them move towards the future they actually want and is an extremely powerful tool for the individual to have.

At this point it is worth making one or two general observations regarding sub-modalities and their uses.

1. Most people are blissfully unaware that they use sub-modalities.
2. Within 15–30 minutes they become fascinated, intrigued and start to see a whole host of uses in all aspects of their lives.
3. If someone doesn't like moving sub-modalities around:
    (a) They don't have to, it's their choice.
    (b) Sub-modalities can always be put back into their original positions should someone want this to be done.

Here are two other examples of sub-modalities exercises.

Exercise 1
Using the list of sub-modalities on pages 186–7, choose a happy experience, go inside and access the states. Play around with changing the sub-modalities, eg:

-   associated/disassociated: move from one to the other;
-   location: move to another location;
-   distance: move from far away to close;
-   colour: vary the colours from intense colours to black and white;
-   size: move from large to small;
-   brightness: move from bright to dull;
-   movement: change from still to slide to film;
-   speed: move from fast to slow;
-   clarity: move from clear to fuzzy;
-   decoration: vary from permanent to quiet and fragmented;
-   depth: move from three to two dimensional;
-   frame/panorama.

Having done this with the visual sub-modalities the same can then be done with the auditory and kinesthetic ones.

This is great practice for finding out about the sub-modalities, moving them around and making positive use of them. It's also great fun.

Exercise 2
One other exercise that makes great use of sub-modalities is called the SWISH. This exercise was developed by Richard Bandler, one of the co-originators of NLP, and it can be used for almost anything. In the learning context it can be used for changing learning habits as it reprogrammes the brain's automatic pilot to move in a new direction, and it can have a profound effect on self-image and esteem.

This exercise can be done alone or in a two or three, following these key steps.

1. Identify a learning situation where the person is stuck, where a different response would make the learning more positive.
2. The person identifies and sees what they would be seeing if they were in the situation. They notice the negative learning behaviour and reproduce all the features, sounds and feelings that go with it. Do this in an associated state.
3. The person now creates a second picture of how they would see themselves if they had already accomplished the desired change, eg being in a positive learning state. Keep making changes to the picture until it's really working well. Do this in a disassociated state.
4. Get the first (negative) picture to be as big and bright as possible. Place a smaller, darker image in the second (positive picture) in the bottom right hand corner.
5. Get the second (positive) picture to grow bigger and brighter and grow to cover the first (negative) picture so that the first picture gets dim and shrinks away. This to happen as fast as the person can say '*swish*'. The faster this happens the better, although speed can be developed with practice.
6. Blank out the screen and do step 4 again, at least five times, taking only one second on each occasion and blanking between each time it is done.
7. At this stage the person can either:
   (a) do a future pace; or
   (b) try to recreate the first picture – if the SWISH has worked this will be difficult, because it will look or feel different. If it is the same, go through the steps again; or
   (c) recreate the external cues. If the old behaviour is still there go through the steps again.

The benefit of this exercise is that it is being used to change a negative learning behaviour by changing the feelings that are attached to the memory. It is also very powerful because it is generative and stacks anchors, each repetition embedding the anchor even more. If this exercise is carried out with two or more people, the observer should be able to see many different changes in physiology.

Other interesting uses for sub-modalities related to topics covered elsewhere in this book are:

- as part of the structure of strategies;
- as part of the structure of values and beliefs.

In fact sub-modalities are the essence of all human experience – helping learners to understand their purpose and uses can really help them make great progress.

Very occasionally someone finds it hard to relate to sub-modalities and may even go so far as to say that they don't have them, or possibly that they don't believe in them. Questions that are useful should this occur are:

- How do you know what is important?
- How do you know *what* you like/don't like?
- How do you know what you believe in?
- How do you know *who* you like/don't like?
- Where do you store the experiences in life that taught you something?

The response to any of these questions can be 'I just know'. A recent example was on a social occasion when someone was being very forceful on the types of music they did or did not like. When asked how they knew they replied, 'I just know, it's instinctive.' Within ten minutes they found that they stored music they liked in a totally different way to the music they didn't, something they had never even considered.

As ever the question is, how can the effective trainer make use of these skills and insights? After all they are not training people in NLP.

The answer is that everything learners do is based upon sub-modalities. Therefore recognition of this, and the willingness to try something new, is an immensely valuable tool. The other part of the answer is of course that they can use it first on themselves and their own experiences.

Some recent examples of how sub-modalities can be used are listed below.

- A senior manager on a selection interviewing course, who felt he knew what the most effective probing questions were was amazed to find out how he 'knew'.
- A difficult and unwilling attendee on a training course, who over coffee mentioned he was trying hard not to eat chocolate but failing. This person was put through the compulsion blow out where the key sub-modalities are exaggerated 20 times and couldn't face a chocolate biscuit for the rest of the week. This changed the dynamics for the whole course for everyone, not just the person in question.

USING SUB-MODALITIES: EXERCISES

1. Use the establishing sub-modalities exercise covered in the section.
2. Use the apathy to motivated exercise covered in the section.
3. Use the wishing to wanting exercise mentioned in this section.
4. Use the happy experience exercise.
5. Experiment with sub-modalities in a variety of training contexts.

USING SUB-MODALITIES: KEY POINTS

☐ Sub-modalities are the 'language of the brain'.
☐ The brain stores and uses information based on sub-modalities.
☐ Sub-modalities are sub-divisions of the five representation systems:
  – visual;
  – auditory;
  – kinesthetic;
  – olfactory;
  – gustatory.
☐ There are clearly defined sub-modalities.
☐ The exercises will help establish sub-modalities for the trainer and learners.
☐ Sub-modalities can be changed (or not), there is a choice.
☐ Sub-modalities can always be put back where they started from.
☐ Sub-modality exercises are generative, ie the more they are done the better they get.
☐ Use the wishing to wanting or SWISH process, or apathy to motivated exercises, if appropriate.
☐ Sub-modalities apply to all aspects of human experience including strategies, values and beliefs:
☐ There are questions that can be asked to help learners who are unsure about sub-modalities.
  – How do you know what is important?
  – How do you know *what* you like/don't like?
  – How do you know what you believe in?
  – How do you know *who* you like/don't like?
  – Where do you store the experiences in life that taught you something?

4.25 USING MEMORY TECHNIQUES

This particular skill comes into the category of 'learning how to learn'. Many learners have disempowering beliefs about their ability to learn *per se*, or their ability to learn a particular topic. These can be rooted in parental upbringing, or an unhappy or difficult situation at school. Quite often the learner does not consciously remember a particular incident or process, but the impact stays with them every time they come up against a similar situation. The NLP processes can be used to help develop a more effective strategy for remembering.

One of the many advantages of demonstrably being able to do something about a so-called 'bad memory' is that it provides a significant reference experience as well as moving a disempowering belief into an empowering one. The power of this is that this positive, forward momentum can then be applied to any other issue or skill that needs to be tackled.

In developing a more effective memory people will have already developed their own personal effectiveness strategies for memory. Children for example are highly kinesthetic, most of their learning comes from touch or a combination of touch with the other senses. Anyone who has watched children at play, a prime learning experience, will have recognized how being able to touch the building blocks, place them on top of each other, or in different shapes and patterns, then knock them all down again, is a crucial part of their learning development. Another aspect is their desire to be touched or kissed after they have done something, to reassure them and show them that everything is all right. They also run around and use up huge amounts of energy in learning, which is another aspect of kinesthetic experience.

The downside to these learning experiences is that normally early in their formal schooling they are 'trained' to sit still, learn by more passive methods, and that, while play is important, it is something separate and different and not related to learning.

At this point children normally develop either a visual or auditory strategy for learning. For example, in learning the multiplication tables they may well do it by rote and only know the answer to 6×8 or 9×7 by either going all the way through the process, saying $1 \times 6 = 6$, $2 \times 6 = 12$, etc to themselves, or as they get faster, start at $4 \times 8 = 32$, $5 \times 8 = 40$, ie they use the same process but with short cuts.

There is also the stage in learning the alphabet where children start right at the beginning, even if the question is 'What comes after Q?', before they can arrive at the correct answer.

These strategies tend to be auditory and once in place will stay for ever. A more visual strategy is to see the information, normally up and to the left, in blocks, if it is a small amount of information, and just pick out the appropriate part. Thus children who, quite naturally, use a predominantly visual strategy, will quite often be seen as quick learners, whereas the more auditory will be recognized as slightly slower but likely to be more accurate and more thorough.

Many children who have learning disabilities are actually doing it in their own particular way, which may not be appropriate to that particular situation. Dependent upon the skills of the parents and their teachers the whole process in learning can be made easier or more difficult.

The capacity to remember

Current research indicates that there may not be any specified limit to the amount people can remember. In addition, speed of acquiring information seems not to be a factor either, the brain can absorb information at amazing speeds, the difficult part is ensuring that accurate retention and recall can take place, at the appropriate time.

Most conventional teaching is based upon traditional approaches rather than helping people to learn to learn, and helping them to learn in a user-friendly way. Unfortunately, as various research has shown, this means that learners' ability to retain and recall is extremely limited. The key pieces of research are summarized here.

The work carried out by the German philosopher Hermann Ebbinghaus in the 1870s was based upon the capacity to remember sets of meaningless syllables. This work showed the following results.

Time from when first learnt	Percentage remembered
20 minutes	53
1 day	38
2 days	31
5 days	25
31 days	22

One observation based upon this research indicates that most forgetting actually occurs *immediately* after the learning input.

This work was followed up by Spitzer who did some similar work, but this time based upon remembering or forgetting material learnt from a textbook. His conclusions were:

Time from when first learnt	Percentage remembered
1 day	54
7 days	35
14 days	21
21 days	19
28 days	18
63 days	17

So how does the brain make sense of information and how is it then able to bring it back accurately and when it is required?

Wyatt Woodsmall, who has done some very useful work in this area, makes the following points (Woodsmall, 1990).

Point 1
The brain finds it easier to remember nouns rather than abstract concepts, eg *brick* is easier to remember than *goodness*, *ladder* is easier to remember than *worthiness*.

Point 2
The brain likes to be able to classify things together, eg *cricket, football, squash, hockey, polo, riding, motor car racing, athletics* are easier to remember under the heading of *sports*.

Point 3

The more time that is put into normal subjects, the greater will be the recall. The exception is the statement, event or set of circumstances which become permanently embedded after only one experience, ie a reference experience.

Point 4

Most learners find it easier to learn in short, sharp, focused bursts, a point a number of trainers have not yet fully taken aboard. This does not mean that sessions need to be shorter, but does mean that they need to be structured in a different way. This will involve more planned breaks and appropriate relaxation.

Point 5

The brain naturally prefers learning to mirror life. For example, when we learn to speak our native language we learn to speak it first and then to apply the correct grammar. Yet many people have learnt foreign languages by trying to learn the grammar first, which has set them up with all sorts of disempowering beliefs regarding their abilities to learn languages.

Point 6

The brain is a meaning making mechanism, that is why the visual aspect can be so useful in helping people develop more effective memories. Remembering things in sentences, classifications.

Point 7

The primary effect can come into play, ie the first, or the first two or three topics or pieces of information can be remembered.

Point 8

In a normal pattern the oddest fact can be the one that sticks out and is retained and recalled. For example, in a list of countries like *France, England, Spain, Portugal, Germany, Poland, Italy,* if *Zanzibar* is put into the middle of the list, a larger number of people will remember *Zanzibar* than the other countries, because it has exotic imagery and implications.

Point 9

As part of these processes the brain will put information into 'chunks'. The trainer needs to help learners have chunks of the right size and the right amount.

Point 10

The brain likes to make sense of information by putting it into a context or situation.

Point 11

Moving information from short-term to long-term memory requires a short period of time. Normally this takes from a few seconds to 15 minutes. This can be done by individual work, syndicate work or getting people to talk the information out loud.

Point 12

Although there is no evidence that people actually learn in their sleep, there is evidence that sleeping time is vital in terms of sorting and processing the information. Significant results have been achieved by getting learners to do a quick review immediately before sleep and then checking it first thing in the morning.

Point 13

Because the brain operates by association, it is very powerful in making the connection between the new and the old information. This works particularly well where it can be made into a story, metaphor or connected series of images.

This means there are certain key techniques of which the effective trainer needs to take note.

- Learners tend to remember what stands out, eg the humorous, bizarre, wacky.
- Learners tend to remember tasks that haven't been completed. This can lead to higher recall, because the brain can't close the door on a topic it views as not completed.
- Learners learn by examples and they also retain them for longer.
- Learners need to be able to review regularly.

Here is one approach used by many NLP trainers and set up on courses for learners to use back at work.

1. Get people to learn material; and give opportunity for immediate practice.
2. After half a day review for ten minutes.
3, After one day review for ten minutes.
4. After one week review for five minutes.
5. After one month review for five minutes.
6. After six months review for five minutes.

The evidence is that, compared with no review at all, this process will aid retention and recall by 400–500 per cent.

It is worth looking briefly at what causes people to forget. The major cause of forgetting is other things getting in the way, or blockages; therefore, the more people know the more they are capable of forgetting, if it has no meaning for them.

Wyatt Woodsmall quotes four types of blockage.

- Retroactive – this is where new learning blocks the recall of previous learning.
- Proactive – this is where old learning blocks the recall of new learning.
- Interactive – this is where older and newer learning block the recall of intermediate learning.
- Reactive – this is where a negative attitude interferes with the recall of learning.

Therefore, the key to effective learning and positive memories is to learn it effectively in the beginning. It must be understood in all systems at all levels in short-term memory first of all, and then through rehearsal and reinforcement moved into long-term memory.

Short-term memory

This is temporary storage and is the most used part of the memory. It converts the words used at the beginning of sentences and holds them long enough to make sense of the whole sentence.

Long-term memory

This is the place where permanent memories take place and is based upon the learning having meaning. It is also able to utilize the learning into a variety of situations, which is the key to most effective learning.

A well known model shows this process as illustrated in Figure 4.4.

Figure 4.4 *Memory model*

Specific ways of learning how to develop better memory

There are many ways to help develop a better memory and the NLP processes will help in all of these.

Mental visualization
This works most effectively when there is an unusual or bizarre connection. For example:

1. Choose five or six random words, practise linking them with the most unusual visual images you can muster. The more unusual the image the more powerful this technique is; trust the right side of the brain.
2 Choose 12–15 random words. Do as above, but add in a story that connects them all together, no matter how silly or stupid the connection seems.

Memory pegs
This relies upon there being a standard image that goes with a number. The generally accepted sequence for one to ten is:

one	bun
two	shoe
three	tree
four	door
five	hive
six	sticks
seven	heaven
eight	gate
nine	wine
ten	hen

As can be seen this process is based upon rhymes. The procedure then is to:

1. Put in the items or information that need to be remembered, eg:

one	lorry
two	paperweight
three	bird
four	telescope
five	igloo
six	biology
seven	car
eight	field
nine	tape
ten	book

2. Then put them together, eg:

one	bun	lorry
two	shoe	paperweight
three	tree	bird
four	door	telescope
five	hive	igloo
six	sticks	biology
seven	heaven	car
eight	gate	field
nine	wine	tape
ten	hen	book

In remembering the lorry all the learner has to do is remember the connection with one – the bun, and the memory of the lorry will happen automatically.

Providing that learners have embedded the original prompts well enough they will find it almost impossible to forget the item to be remembered.

This technique is sometimes used by trainers at the beginning of a training event and is a spectacular way of proving a point by remembering 50 items in ten minutes. Its best use is to help learners develop their own learning strategies, which they can then apply for themselves.

This version is both visual and auditory and is, therefore, very powerful. Another version is to use the numbers but rather than use a rhyme just use a visual image that relates to the number of the item to be remembered, eg one can be the image of a stick; two, a skier; three, two hills on their side; four, a key. If these images do not make any sense it may well be because the reader is not visual.

Another similar process can be used for remembering names and faces. Again it can be a useful and dynamic way to start a training programme, while at the same time equipping people with an ongoing skill, which they can use in a variety of situations.

This process can be used with either forenames and/or family names and involves learning the name of the other person and associating the first image that comes to mind, prompted by the name, eg Harley could be a motorbike, Garratt could be an artist starving in a loft, Richard could be lionheart, etc.

Applying this to faces involves looking for a distinctive feature and allying that to the associated name, eg John Ford with a moustache could be a toilet floating in water with a man's face with a moustache painted on it. This sounds very cumbersome but once embedded is unforgettable. Sometimes, when there isn't an image that comes to mind, the association can be based on the sounds in the name, eg Mendelssohn can be a sewing job in a leafy dell with your, or someone's, son. The key thing is that the image needs to be strong and vibrant.

Mnemonics

Virtually every child has at some point used mnemonics to help them remember crucial information. Most of these can be remembered throughout adult life as well, in fact they are impossible to forget.

Some examples are:

Richard of York gave battle in vain
 – for the colours of the rainbow.

Every good boy deserves fruit
 – for musical notes.

Thirty days hath September
April, June and November
All the rest have thirty-one
Excepting February alone
Which has twenty-eight days clear
Except in a leap year it has one day more
 – for the days in the month.

I before *E*, except after *C*
 – as a spelling strategy.

All of these are very common, are based on forms and stick forever.

Anchors

One of the key tools in NLP and one that can be applied to all aspects of learning. Creating positive anchors for learning makes a huge difference. One use of anchors is to help learners take away the learning rather than leaving it anchored in the training room.

Sub-modalities

One fun and useful way to get people into sub-modalities is to use them to help show learners how they store information and memories. The advantage of this is that learning is taking place on more than one topic at more than one level at the same time.

Metaphors

Metaphors are very useful, and in the context of developing a better memory have a distinct role to play, particularly if the metaphor 'belongs' to the learner.

Most NLP techniques can be applied in some way to assist the development of a better memory. In fact using a range of NLP techniques can make learning fun while giving learners a positive reference experience.

A lot of time and attention has been devoted to the memory, and like all of the techniques used in this book, it can be used on at least two levels:

1. for the trainers themselves;
2. for the positive benefit of the learners.

Again it is useful for the trainer to be able to show, by their own personal excellence, that they are 'walking what they are talking'.

USING MEMORY TECHNIQUES: EXERCISES

1. Use mental visualization.
2. Use memory pegs.
3. Use combination of 1 and 2.
4. Use mnemonics.
5. Use anchors.
6. Use sub-modalities.
7. Use metaphors.
8. Combine with other relevant NLP skills and techniques, eg creating positive beliefs, creating reference experiences, changing learner states, being aware of invisibles.

USING MEMORY TECHNIQUES: KEY POINTS

☐ Developing a good memory is 'learning to learn'.
☐ Bad learning can create disempowering beliefs.
☐ Much learning is by rote.
☐ Most learning is lost early on.
☐ The brain remembers by one or more of the following points:
  – nouns rather than abstracts;
  – the brain likes to classify;
  – time is a factor;
  – learners prefer short bursts;
  – learning should mirror life;
  – the brain likes to make meaning;
  – the primary effect may happen;
  – the oldest fact or the most exotic can be the one that sticks:
  – the brain likes to chunk;
  – the brain likes to put information into a situation or context;
  – it is important to move information from short- to long-term memory;
  – review takes place before sleep and again in the morning;
  – the brain likes to make associations.
☐ Learners remember what is humorous, bizarre, wacky.
☐ Learners tend to remember what hasn't been completed.
☐ Learners learn by example.

□ Learners react to regularly review.
□ Use the review process:
  – Learn material.
  – After half day – review ten minutes.
  – After one day – review ten minutes.
  – After one week – review five minutes.
  – After one month – review five minutes.
  – After six months – review five minutes.
□ Remember the four types of blockage:
  – retroactive;
  – proactive;
  – interactive;
  – reactive.
□ Help learners move from short- to long-term memory.
□ Use a variety of ways to help learners learn:
  – mental visualization;
  – memory pegs;
  – mnemonics;
  – anchors;
  – sub-modalities;
  – metaphors.

4.26 USING PRESENT STATE – DESIRED STATE

The output from most training (and from many other interactions) is a move from present to desired state. In NLP terms these can be defined as:

Present state – an undesirable state where an individual lacks the resources or knowledge to change to a more positive state.

Desired state – a positive psychological/physiological state of excellence.

It is worth pointing out that these definitions can also apply to groups and teams as well. It is also important to note that most real changes may occur after the desired state has been achieved, not just in achieving the desired state. Therefore, for training to bring about a desired change there is almost certainly going to be a move from present to desired state. Many individuals, groups, teams and organizations are very good at articulating the present (unresourced) state, but less clear about where they want to be. In Meta Program terms they are moving away rather than moving toward, and looking at necessity not possibility. Helping them by using the outcomes process is a powerful way of assisting them to move forward. All of the NLP exercises in this book can help a move from present to desired state.

USING PRESENT – DESIRED STATE: EXERCISES

1. Use the outcomes process to clarify and agree the desired state.
2. Use any of the appropriate NLP skills and techniques covered in this book.
3. Run a session on present – desired state as part of a training, eg on a self-motivation or team building programme.

USING PRESENT – DESIRED STATE: KEY POINTS

☐ Most training is about a move from present to desired state.
☐ Some change can occur after the desired state has been achieved (you could call this Desired State 2, 3, etc).
☐ Many individuals, groups, teams and organizations move away from rather than move toward and base their strategy on necessity not possibility.
☐ The NLP outcomes process helps achieve moving toward the desired state.

USING PRESENT – DESIRED STATE: CASE STUDY

A participant 'sent' on a personal change programme was visibly unhappy about his capacity to change. He was very clear regarding his present state, and all the negative issues that went with it, but less clear on what the desired state could be.

By a process of Meta Model questions, artfully vague language, calibration with a little bit of Meta Programs and timelines, it was possible to clarify the desired state.

This was then put into the outcomes process. The physiological and language pattern differences evidenced by the participant were visible to everyone else on the programme. The difference this made to the individual and other participants became a key factor in the ongoing success of the programme.

4.27 USING EDITS

Edits are one of the newer parts of NLP (sometimes called the new code) and are based on work by John Grinder, one of the original co-developers of NLP. They are another way to help learners add to or feel more resourceful and, therefore, fit in with present state – desired state. There are a variety of edits which a trainer can use either on themselves or to help learners. For the purposes of this book two will suffice.

USING EDITS: EXERCISES

These exercises can be done alone, but do benefit from working with a partner. If working with a partner, the partner does not get involved with content, ie the actual issue. Their role is to help the person with the issue maintain maximum physiology.

1. Personal Edit – Breathing
   - Identify a choice point, this is an area where you want to change, or make a difference in your life, eg some aspect of learning. Do this from the third (coach) perceptual position.
   - Do an internal congruency check to ensure that you know it's OK to proceed. This would normally be based on a kinesthetic response.
   - Access and inventory the choice point (this means accessing the state and checking everything out with regard to VAKOG and any other representations, eg sub-modalities).
   - Break state.
   - Choose the posture and position that best relates to the choice point posture. Then from your past choose a reference experience which worked, and re-access all the physiology and feelings that went with the reference experience, in particular the breathing.
   - If working with a partner the partner memorizes and calibrates to the breathing pattern of the experience that worked using VAKOG.
   - Then, taking the physiology, breathing pattern and VAKOG representations of the experience that worked (associated), think through the original choice point.
   - Ensure that the physiology, breathing and VAKOG representations are maintained throughout (if working with a partner their role is to help you achieve this).
   - Carry on doing this until a purposeful change has occurred to the choice point.
2. Characterological Adjectives – this is a quick, fun exercise which works extremely effectively, and is based upon the use of perceptual positions (see 2.7, page 48).
   - Think of someone you know with whom you would like to achieve a change.
   - Imagine a stage with that person and yourself on it, with you in third position in the audience, watching and listening to the two people on the stage.
   - Describe the behaviour, from third position in the audience, by using an adjective of the person you would like to achieve a change with.
   - Then turn up the stage lights on the other part of the stage to illuminate the you that is on the stage.
   - Be aware of what the you on the stage is doing with regard to the other person.
   - Describe the behaviour of the you on the stage from third position in the audience, by using an adjective.

- Ask – What have I been doing in the past that has ensured that the other person carried on carrying out their behaviour?

  This shifts the emphasis from wanting the other person to change to recognizing that it is our behaviour that allows or encourages them to behave in the way that they do. Therefore, we have created a circle in which you do something, therefore they do something, and so it goes on.

A further step in this process can be:

- What advice would the you, in third position in the audience, give to the you on the stage to help the you on the stage change behaviour, thereby breaking the circle?

Additionally, of course, having done all this it can be followed by a future pace.

USING EDITS: KEY POINTS

☐ Edits are part of the newer developments in NLP.
☐ They add to resources or make people feel more resourceful.
☐ There are a variety of edits which can be used as well as the ones covered in the exercises.

USING EDITS: CASE STUDY

In a mentoring session with a director of a service organization, it was apparent how easily he became unresourced and drifted away from being able to take responsibility for his own development. When reviewing the changes he had chosen to tackle he revisited past experiences and became weighed down with the difficulties of personal change and his capacity to make the necessary changes.

In analysing past issues it became apparent that he had achieved successes, but had managed to delete or distort them, and thereby make them negative.

At no stage in the mentoring process had NLP been mentioned or discussed, but it was obvious that he was stuck and making it harder for himself. Rather than try to explain what NLP was and how it worked, it was decided to use the Breathing edit as part of a normal conversation. This was done and the participant became more focused and resourced, leaving the meeting ready to tackle key issues.

At the next meeting he was able to report on some successes and also commented on how much better he felt about the whole process. At this stage the Breathing edit was explained to him and where it fitted in to NLP. As he had already had a positive experience he was more intrigued than if it were dry theory, and he asked for more information on NLP. Subsequently he became trained in NLP and now uses a number of its processes on himself to aid his further development.

4.28 USING THE NEW BEHAVIOUR GENERATOR

The new behaviour generator is one of the best-known processes in the whole of NLP. It can be used in a huge variety of situations and is a process for achieving a behavioural change for yourself. It is based on using the three main representation systems to develop the new behaviour required. One of the reasons that it works so effectively is that the unconscious mind cannot tell the difference between something that has been imagined, in a particularly vivid way, and something that has actually taken place. This helps explain why some dreams and memories become 'real' to people.

This process takes this point and optimizes it to achieve a new behaviour or to change a behaviour that is no longer helpful or purposeful. It is, therefore, very useful for trainers to be able to use for themselves or to assist learners.

USING THE NEW BEHAVIOUR GENERATOR: EXERCISES

1. Choose the specific behaviour you want to change and develop or have for the first time.
2. Ask 'How would I look, sound and feel if I were carrying out this behaviour effectively?' Imagine yourself doing it in the specific situation you want. Live the whole in all your senses. (If for some reason you cannot see, hear and feel yourself doing the behaviour, imagine someone you know who is good at it, or even someone from a movie or TV programme – the key point is that any form of representation will help and assist the process.)
3. If there is something that isn't right, keep running it through, making any necessary changes, and keep doing this until it is working for you, you are performing as you want to be.
4. When the imagined performance is working for you, go inside that image of yourself doing the behaviour effectively, ie become associated.
5. As you run it through an associated state, be in tune with all the feelings of yourself and others that go with it.
6. If, for some reason, you need to modify any aspect of your behaviour, step out (become disassociated) make the necessary adjustments, then step back in again (associated) and check it out.
7. Ask yourself 'How will I know by seeing, hearing or feeling, that it is the right time to use the new behaviour?' – decide on the signal.
8. Imagine that the signal has happened, you have used your new behaviour, it has worked, be aware of how you feel.

USING THE NEW BEHAVIOUR GENERATOR: KEY POINTS

☐ One of the best-known processes in NLP.
☐ A process for achieving behavioural change.
☐ Can be used for new behaviours or to modify existing ones.
☐ Based on the unconscious mind not knowing the difference between a real and a vividly imagined event.
☐ Can be used by the trainer on themselves or with learners.

USING THE NEW BEHAVIOUR GENERATOR: CASE STUDY

This case study took place over a lunch break on a training programme, when a conversation developed about personal change and how it could be applied in non-work situations. The individual who raised the issue was a squash player who felt that he had 'plateaued' and, although still trying hard, was not getting anywhere. The specific comment was 'no matter what I do I still keep making the same old mistakes'. He had also paid to have coaching, but felt that this had merely made him even more aware of his shortcomings.

He was asked if he was prepared to try a quick, fun approach which he could then use by himself. No explanation about NLP was given, just the process itself. Ten minutes later he was chuckling and very animated regarding what had taken place.

Since that time he believes that the quality of his squash has improved, and that he is now achieving better results than previously. He has also started to use the process in other areas of his life.

4.29 USING INTERNAL DIALOGUE

One of the jokes within NLP is that people used to be burnt at the stake for hearing voices and seeing things. Now with NLP it's all legitimate!

Internal dialogue can best be described at the 'inner voice' that people have, that no one else ever hears. For many people it is used in a negative way, eg to self-discount, to create anxiety, to add to stress, to chide. Some psychologists contend that about 70 per cent of someone's internal dialogue can be negative.

Most people have also been woken in the middle of the night by their internal dialogue reminding them or telling them something. In mental preparation for sports, many sports people mention 'interference factors', ie the things that pop into the mind when least required to distract and confuse. On training courses most people acknowledge this and quote stories about how they tell themselves how hard something is, or tell themselves everyone else seems to understand the subject better than they do.

The issue, therefore, is to substitute positive internal dialogue for negative and learning can be a good place to start. Eastern mystics actually study specifically to utilize their internal dialogue in a positive way, and many sports stars have developed positive internal dialogue as well to help overcome the 'interference factors'.

USING INTERNAL DIALOGUE: EXERCISES

1. Use affirmations.
2. Use autogenics.
3. Use mental rehearsal.
4. Use appropriate NLP techniques, eg perceptual positions, new behaviour generation, timelines, the ten day challenge.
5. Practise interrupting any negative internal dialogue with more positive messages.
6. Meta Model your negative internal dialogue.

USING INTERNAL DIALOGUE: KEY POINTS

☐ Internal dialogue is the inner voice that people hear.
☐ For many people their internal dialogue is negative, self-discounting, etc.
☐ Many learners have negative internal dialogue regarding training.
☐ It is helpful to develop positive internal dialogue.

CONFIRMING THE LEARNING

5

CONFIRMING THE LEARNING

'Experience is not what you do, it's what you do with what you do.'
Aldous Huxley

Having gone through the training it is vital to complete the training loop and ensure that the learning has been completed. This step, although obvious, is sometimes not carried out, or only carried out superficially. This can leave the learner either confused and demoralized or hyped up in an unrealistic way when they go back to work.

5.1 REVISING OBJECTIVES

This may seem an odd step to have to take and often it won't be necessary. Sometimes, even though the objectives/expectations have been agreed between the organization, the trainer and the learners, for a variety of reasons something different occurs, something else is achieved, or some objectives are not met.

Therefore, it is important for all concerned that the actual objectives agreed are revised and updated. This assumes particular importance when the learners are going back to a situation where their managers believe that one set of objectives has been achieved, when something different may have happened.

This is where using the NLP outcomes process and the other NLP skills can assist. The outcomes process to revisit the objectives, and the other skills, eg sensory acuity, reframing, dealing with invisibles, all show learners how to make the best use of what they have learned and how best to apply it. In addition, using the outcomes process in the first place can help ensure that the original objectives are actually achieved.

REVISING OBJECTIVES: EXERCISES

1. Use the NLP outcomes process to establish objectives.
2. Use NLP skills to assist in achievement of objectives.
3. Revise objectives where necessary.

REVISING OBJECTIVES: KEY ACTIONS

☐ Objectives need to be agreed by organization, trainer and learner.
☐ Sometimes different objectives are achieved.
☐ Sometimes the original objectives are not achieved.
☐ Use NLP outcomes process.
☐ Use the full range of appropriate NLP skills.

REVISING OBJECTIVES: CASE STUDY

A training programme on implementing a new performance management process had been designed and run. The agreed objectives had been achieved with the exception of one regarding the role of the 'grandfather' figure, which all the participants felt was not going to be used to its best purpose.

The Human Resources manager had been adamant that the original objectives should be achieved, while the participants felt he was forcing the point for other reasons. In discussing the issue with him during the course review session, his discomfort was evident to all.

In using Meta Model questions, calibration and matching language patterns, his real concerns were discovered. He was concerned about the credibility of the HR function in senior management's eyes. Having established the real issue a 'win-win' message, based on the *actual* learnings, was agreed for him to take back to senior management.

5.2 AGREEING ACTION PLANS

The output from any training and from using NLP skills and techniques should normally be ongoing action. This can be established either by the learner, by and for themselves, or in conjunction with the trainer and/or the line manager or HR manager.

All trainers will have their own ways of documenting and agreeing action plans. Many of the NLP skills can be used to aid this process; they are of particular relevance as they allow learners to take responsibility for their own development and equip them with the skills to do so.

AGREEING ACTION PLANS: EXERCISES

Use appropriate NLP skills and techniques, eg creating rapport, changing learner states, new behaviour generator, present – desired state, creating positive beliefs, anchors, future pace.

AGREEING ACTIONS PLANS: KEY POINTS

☐ Training should create ongoing action.
☐ Action can be self, trainer and/or line manager driven.
☐ Many NLP processes can be used to help.
☐ Equip learners with skills to manage own learning.

5.3 USING CHECKLISTS

Checklists are a standard part of the trainers' repertoire. Normally they are pre-prepared and used as handouts. One additional strategy is to get individuals and groups to prepare their own checklists. This allows them to practise whatever skills have been taught on the programme and evidence suggests that greater use will be made of something that is self- (rather than trainer-) generated.

USING CHECKLISTS: EXERCISES

1. Get learners to prepare their own checklists either individually or in groups.
2. Get them to use NLP skills to help them do this.
3. Get them to anchor and future pace use of checklists.

USING CHECKLISTS: KEY POINTS

☐ Normal part of trainers' repertoire.
☐ Learners developing their own ensures greater chance of use after the programme.

USING CHECKLISTS: CASE STUDY

When carrying out the end of course review at the end of a selection interviewing course, one learner expressed a concern that while he had benefited from the training, he was unsure that he would remember to 'do the right thing at the right time'. This theme was also then picked up on by other delegates.

Each delegate was asked to choose two key skills from the checklist to work on, then the anchoring and future pace processes carried out (again without mentioning NLP until after they had done the process, when they wanted to know more). Subsequent feedback indicated that the key actions from the checklists had been carried out.

5.4 EFFECTIVE ENDINGS

Earlier in this book we talked about topics such as creating and maintaining high expectations, creating rituals and engaging emotions. These obviously help to start the training in the right way.

Equally, finishing on a clear, positive, focused note, helps ensure that:

- the training itself finishes successfully;
- the learning will be taken and transferred after the course has finished.

EFFECTIVE ENDINGS: EXERCISES

1. Use ritual goodbyes.
2. Get everyone to share three things they are going away to work on.
3. Finish with a future pace.
4. Finish with a timeline.
5. Finish with a symbolic (to the group) piece of music.
6. Finish with a visualization.
7. Use a mindmap to finish.
8. Finish by applauding themselves.
9. Each learner creates a thought/maxim based on the learning.

EFFECTIVE ENDINGS: KEY POINTS

- ☐ Are as, if not more, important than good beginnings.
- ☐ Finish the training event successfully.
- ☐ Help learning be transferred into the future.

EFFECTIVE ENDINGS: CASE STUDY

An outdoor training course was coming to an end. After initial concerns and reservations, participants, who had been sent, had become fully involved and committed. During the course, which had involved all the usual outdoor activities, one of the trainers had taken a series of photographs of all the key (and amusing) incidents.

These were developed over lunchime on the last day, and a set created for each participant. As part of the end of the course each person was given a set of photographs. They then chose one from their set which captured the key point of the training *as far as they were concerned*, developed a thought/maxim based on the picture and put it up on a flipchart.

This montage was then photographed and circulated after the course as a memento and reminder. In addition, a piece of music and course motto was agreed and anchors established to assist in implementation back at work.

5.5 POST-COURSE SELF-EVALUATION

Every trainer will have outcomes for a training and some of these should be specific to the trainer and their development, rather than just based on the learners. For example, working on creating rapport, developing the ability to use third position, recognizing Meta Programs. This keeps trainers fresh and also helps them become more effective for the learners they work with.

After the training is completed, the trainer should review their personal outcomes.

POST-COURSE SELF-EVALUATION: EXERCISES

1. Use outcomes process to establish personal outcomes for the training, based upon using specific NLP skills and techniques.
2. Review personal outcomes and results achieved.
3. Use feedback from reverse tests.

POST-COURSE SELF-EVALUATION: KEY POINTS

☐ Review of personal outcomes should take place.
☐ Personal outcomes should be based on using/developing NLP skills and techniques.
☐ The reverse tests can be used to help self-evaluation.

5.6 LEARNING FOR NEXT TIME

Following on from the post-course self-evaluation process is the learning for next time. The whole point of self-development, which should be every trainer's aim, is to improve, rather than just carrying on doing what has (or has not) worked in the past.

LEARNING FOR NEXT TIME: EXERCISES

1. Having reviewed previous outcomes, establish personal outcomes for the next time, geared to a topic, a session or group.
2. Develop a structured learning plan for a period of three months, then review and update it.
3. Choose some NLP skills and techniques to develop both inside and outside the training format.
4. From the results of the reverse tests chose what to work on and develop.

LEARNING FOR NEXT TIME: KEY POINTS

- ☐ All trainers should aim to self-develop.
- ☐ Establish outcomes for each training.
- ☐ Develop a structured learning plan, review and update it.
- ☐ Work on NLP skills.
- ☐ Use reverse tests to help choose what to work on.

GLOSSARY OF TERMS

*'Education is what you have left after you have forgotten everything you
have ever learned.'*
Anon

Anchoring   The way that a stimulus or representation, which can be either
internal or external, becomes connected to and triggers a response.
Anchors can be established deliberately or occur naturally.

Associated   Being inside one's own experiences and body looking out
from own eyes.

Backtracking   Repeating back exactly what someone has said.

Behaviour modelling   The way of establishing the sequence of thoughts
and behaviours that enable a specific task to be achieved.

Break state   Interrupting what is taking place. Excellent when going from
disassociated to associated.

Calibration   Reading, fine-tuning and being sensitive to a person's or
group's non-verbal behaviour.

Chunking   The ability to change a perception by moving up or down
logical levels. Normally into more or less levels of detail.

Complex equivalence   Two statements that are supposed to mean the
same thing, eg the trainer didn't answer my question, they don't like
me.

Content reframing   Looking at a different part of an experience or
statement to give it another meaning.

Context reframing   Changing the context of an experience or statement
to give it a different meaning.

Cross-over mirroring   Matching one sensory system by use of another,
eg swinging a foot while pacing someone tapping a pencil.

Deletions   Missing out part of an experience in thought or speech.

Desired state   A positive physiological/psychological state of excellence.

Disassociation   Being outside one's own experience and body. Looking
at self as if on a screen.

Distortions Inaccurately representing something in internal experience in a limiting way.

Dominant sensory system The sensory system through which an individual most consciously processes information. Predicate patterns and eye accessing cues give evidence of the dominance.

Downtime Being in a state which is inwardly directed, eg daydreaming, self-preoccupied.

Edits A range of processes designed to change physiology and therefore state to achieve greater choice.

Embedded command Establishing an idea with the unconscious mind.

Eye accessing cues How the eyes move to indicate visual, auditory or kinesthetic thinking.

First position Being aware of the world from your own point of view.

Future pacing Mentally rehearsing a future outcome to help bring it about.

Generalizations Using one specific experience to represent a complete aspect of experience.

Internal dialogue The inner voice that most people conduct internal conversations with and only they hear.

Leading Having rapport with another person, then changing one's own behaviour which the other person follows.

Learning patterns The habitual ways that people prefer to learn.

Left brain/right brain The different ways the two parts of the brain prefer to work, ie left – logical/analytical, right – intuitive, creative.

Logical levels Different levels of experience, environment, behaviour, capability, beliefs, identity.

Matching Subtly responding to one or more of the following: facial expressions, posture, gestures, eye accessing cues, voice tone, tempo, pitch, predicates.

Meta Model A language-based model that obscures meaning by a process of distortion, deletion and generalization, with challenges to restore meanings.

Meta Program The patterns of the way we structure experience through systematic and habitual filters.

Metaphors Anecdotes, parables and stories which, if constructed and used correctly, may result in long-term behavioural change.

Mirroring Matching other people's behaviour to achieve rapport.

Mismatching Using different patterns of behaviour that break rapport.

New behaviour generator An NLP technique modifying, adapting or establishing a new behaviour.

Non-verbal communication The subtle but significant level of body language, eg skin colour, pupil dilation, swallowing.

Outcomes A specific sensory-based desired result that meets the criteria of well formedness.

Perceptual positions   Different viewpoints, as in first, second or third position.

Predicates   Adjectives, verbs, adverbs and other descriptive words, which give evidence of a representational systems preference.

Present state   An undesirable state where an individual lacks the resources or knowledge to change to a more positive state.

Pre-suppositions   Words or statements that establish a future event, eg *when* this training course is over.

Rapport   Entering another person's world. Respectfully mirroring physiology and non-verbals as well as language patterns.

Reference experience   A significant event that stays with the person for a long time, to which they attach great meaning and significance.

Reframing   Changing the frame of reference in a situation to give it another meaning.

Representation system   The coding people use for sensory information, visual, auditory, kinesthetic, olfactory, gustatory.

Second position   Seeing things from another person's point of view.

Sensory acuity   The ability to be aware of sensory feedback.

Sleight of mouth   How people make content or context reframes for particular belief statements.

Strategies   A sequence of thought and behaviour that achieves a certain outcome.

Sub-modalities   The components that make up each modality or representation system. They enable the brain to sort and code our experience, eg the size and brightness of an internal image.

Swish pattern   A sub-modality pattern that programmes the brain in a specific direction.

Third position   Seeing something from the perspective of a detached, external observer, eg the self-coach.

Timeline   The way people represent time by storing pictures of the past, present, future.

Uptime   A state of focused attention, where the senses are focused externally, rather than internally.

Visualization   Being able to see pictures and images in the mind.

BIBLIOGRAPHY

*'Reading is not a duty, and has consequently no business to be made
disagreeable.'*
Augustine Birrell

Abramis, D (1991) 'There is nothing wrong with a little fun', *The San Diego Union,*
March, p.25.
Bandler, R (1985) *Using Your Brain for a Change,* Real People Press, Utah.
Bandler, R and Grinder, J (1975) *The Structure of Magic I,* Science & Behavior Books,
Palo Alto, California.
Bandler, R and Grinder, J (1976) *The Structure of Magic II,* Science & Behavior Books,
Palo Alto, California.
Bandler, R and Grinder, J (1979) *Frogs Into Princes,* Real People Press, Utah.
Bandler, R and Grinder, J (1982) *Reframing, Neuro Linguistic Programming and the
Transformation of Meaning,* Real People Press, Utah.
Bandler, R and McDonald, W (1988) *An Insider's Guide to Sub-Modalities,* Meta
Publications, Capitola, California.
Bandura, A (1986) *Social Foundations of Thought and Action: A Social Cognitive
Theory,* Prentice Hall, Englewood Cliffs, New Jersey.
Botella, J and Eriksen, C W (1992) 'Filtering versus parallel processing in RSVP
tasks', *Perception and Psychophysics,* 51, 4, 334–43.
Brewer, C and Campbell, D (1991) *Rhythms of Learning,* Zephyr Press, Tucson,
Arizona.
Brostrom, R (1979) *Training Style Inventory: 1979 Annual Handbook for Group
Facilitators,* University Associates, San Diego, California.
Buzan, T (1993) *The Mind Map Book,* BBC Books, London.
Caine, R N and Geoffrey, C (1991) *Making Connections: Teaching and The Human
Brain,* Association for Supervision and Curriculum Development, Alexandria,
VA.
Charvet, S R (1996) *Words That Change Minds,* Kendall Hunt Publishing Co,
Dublique, Iowa.
Cleveland, B E (1987) *Master Teaching Techniques,* The Connecting Lines Press,
Lawrenceville, Georgia.
Covey, S (1989) *Seven Habits of Highly Effective People,* Simon & Schuster, London.

Crick, F (1994) *The Astonishing Hypothesis: The Scientific Search for the Soul,* Charles Scribner and Sons, New York.

De Lozier, J (1980) *Neuro Linguistic Programming, Volume I,* Meta Publications, Capitola, California.

Dean, O (1993) 'The effective use of humor in human resource development', in *Developing Human Resources Annual,* University Associates, San Diego, California.

Dilts, R (1990) *Changing Belief Systems with NLP,* Meta Publications, Capitola, California.

Dilts, R (1994) *Effective Presentation Skills,* Meta Publications, Capitola, California.

Dilts, R and Epstein, T (1991) *Tools for Dreamers,* Meta Publications, Capitola, California.

Dilts, R and Epstein, T (1995) *Dynamic Learning,* Meta Publications, Capitola, California.

Dilts, R, Grinder, J, Bandler, R and De Lozier, J (1980) *Neuro Linguistic Programming,* Vol 1, Meta Publications, Capitola, California.

Duncan, W J and Feisal, P (1989) 'No laughing matter: Patterns of humour in the workplace', Organisational Dynamics, 17, 18–30.

Eicher, J (1987) *Making the Message Clear,* Grinder De Lozier Associates, Santa Cruz, California.

Ford, M (1992) *Motivating Humans,* Sage Publications, Newbury Park, California.

Freely, M F (1984) 'An experimental investigation of the relationships among teachers' individual time preferences in service workshop schedules, and instructional techniques and the subsequent implementation of learning style strategies in the participant's classroom', St John's University, Diss.

Gardner, H with Krechevsky, M (1993) *Multiple Intelligences: The Theory in Practice,* Basic Books, New York.

Grinder, M (1991) *Righting the Educational Conveyor Belt,* Metamorphous Press, Portland, Oregon.

Hersey, P and Blanchard, K H (1982) *Management of Organizational Behavior: Utilizing Human Resources,* 4th edn, Prentice Hall, Englewood Cliffs, New Jersey.

Honey, P and Mumford, A (1986) *Learning Styles Questionnaire: Using Your Learning Styles,* Peter Honey, Maidenhead.

Hooper, J and Terisi, D (1986) *The Three Pound Universe: The Brain, from Chemistry of the Mind to New Frontiers of the Soul,* Dell Publishing, New York.

James, T and Woodsmall, W (1988) *Time Line Therapy and The Basis of Personality,* Meta Publications, Capitola, California.

James, T (1989) *The Secret of Creating your Future,* Advanced Neuro Dynamics, Honolulu, Hawaii.

Jensen, E (1994a) *Super-Teaching: Master Strategies for Building Student Success,* Turning Points for Teachers, San Diego, California.

Jensen, E (1994b) *The Learning Brain,* Turning Points for Teachers, San Diego, California.

Kiechell, W III (1983) 'Executives ought to be funnier', *Fortune Magazine,* 12 December, 206–16.

Klein and Armitage (1979) 'Brainwave Cycle Fluctuations', *Science,* 204, 1326–28.

Kolb, David (1976) *Learning Styles Inventory,* McBer & Company, Boston, Massachusetts.

Kostere, K and Malatesta, L (1985) *Get the Results You Want*, Metamorphous Press, Portland, Oregon.

Kostere, K and Malatesta, L (1990) *Maps, Models and the Structure of Reality*, Metamorphous Press, Portland, Oregon.

Kotulak, R (1993) 'Unravelling hidden mysteries of the brain', *Chicago Tribune*, 11–16 April 1993.

Laborde, Genie Z (1984) *Influencing with Integrity*, Syntony Publishing Co, Mountain View, California.

Laborde, Genie Z (1985) *90 Days to Communication Excellence*, Syntony Publishing Co, Palo Alto, California.

Locke, E A and Latham, G P (1990) 'Work motivation and satisfaction: Light at the end of the tunnel' *Psychological Science*, 1, 240–46.

Lozanov, G (1978) *Suggestology and Outlines of Suggestopedy*, Gordon and Breach, New York.

Lozanov, G (1991) 'On some problems of the anatomy, physiology and biochemistry of cerebral activities in the global-artistic approach in modern suggestopedagogic training', *The Journal of the Society for Accelerative Learning and Teaching*, 16, 2, 101–16.

Maguire, J (1990) *Care and Feeding of the Brain*, Doubleday, New York.

McCarthy, B (1981) *4 Mat System*, Excel Inc, Barrintgton, Illinois.

McGaugh, J L (1989) 'Dissociating Learning and Performance: Drug and Hormone Enhancement of Memory Storage', *Brain Research Bulletin*, 23, 4–5.

McGaugh, J L et al. (1990) 'Involvement of the Amygdaloid Complex in Neuromodulatory Influences on Memory Storage', *Neuroscience and Biobehavioural Reviews*, 14.4, 45, 31.

Mehrabian, A (1972) *Nonverbal Communication*, Aldine-Atherton, Chicago and New York.

O'Keefe, J and Nadel, L (1978) *The Hippocampus as a Cognitive Map*, Clarendon Press, Oxford.

Ostrander, S and Schroeder, L with Ostrander, N (1994) *Super Learning 2000*, Souvenir Press, London.

Palmer, J (1994) *Taking Humour Seriously*, Routledge, London.

Price, G (1980) 'Which learning style elements are stable and which tend to change?' *Learning Styles Network Newsletter*, 4, 2, 38–40.

Richardson, J (1988) *The Magic of Rapport*, Meta Publications, Capitola, California.

Robbins, A (1992) *Awakening the Giant Within*, Simon and Schuster, Englewood Cliffs, New Jersey.

Rose, C and Tracy, B (1995) *Accelerated Learning Techniques*, Nightingale Conant, Niles, Illinois.

Seymour, J and O'Connor, J (1990) *Introducing NLP*, HarperCollins, London.

Seymour, J and O'Connor, J (1994) *Training with NLP*, HarperCollins, London.

Sperry, R (1968) 'Disconnection and unity in conscious awareness', *American Psychologist*, 23, 723–33.

Van Nagel, C, Reese, E J, Reese, M and Siudzinski, T (1985) *Mega-Teaching and Learning*, Southern Institute Press, Indian Rock Beach, Florida.

Virotsko, J (1983) 'Analysis of the relationships among academic achievement in mathematics and reading, assigned instructional schedules, and the learning style time preferences of third, fourth, fifth and sixth grade students', St John's University, Diss.

Wheeler, M and Marshall, J (1986) *Trainer Type Inventory (1986) Annual Developing Human Resources*, University Associates, San Diego, California.

Woodsmall, W (1990) *Training for Excellence*, Advanced Neuro Dynamics, Honolulu, Hawaii.

Woodsmall, W and James, T (1988) *Timeline Therapy and the Basis of Personality*, Meta Publications, Capitola, California.

INDEX

accelerated learning 155–61
  case study 161
  exercises 160
  key points 160–61
  key skills 157–8
  NLP in 160
accommodator 11, 134–5
achievements 21
action plans 106, 214–15
active language 21
activist 11, 29, 132
advice 139
ambiguity 73
anchors/anchoring 19–20, 45–8
  case study 48
  exercises 48
  in memory techniques 202
  key points 47, 48
  key steps 46–7
  process 46
artfully vague language 73–4, 76
Ashby's Law of Requisite Variety 5
assimilator 11, 134, 135
association/disassociation 62–4
  case study 64
  exercises 63
  key points 63
associations between experiences
  45–6
attention 28
auditory metaphors 78
auditory predicates 71
auditory style 14
autogenics 159–60

backtracking 85–6

exercises 86
  key points 86
Bandler, Richard 2, 3, 68, 191
Bateson, Gregory 2
behaviour modelling and strategies
  4, 39–44
  case study 41
  exercises 44
  key points 44
behaviour patterns 169
behavioural changes 136–8
  exercises 137
  key points 138
  new behaviour generator 208
behaviourist style 12, 13
belief systems revealed by language
  patterns 74–6
beliefs 127–9
  positive 153
big picture/little picture technique
  54–5
  exercises 55
  key points 55
body language 33
  use of phrase 113
  see also non-verbal communication
BRAC (Break–Rest–Activity Cycle)
  27
brain
  left 57, 59
  right 57, 59
brain hemisphere functions 55–60
  exercises 60
  key points 60
breathing patterns 18
Briggs, Myers 168

Brostrom, R 13
Buzan, Tony 59

calibration 19, 60–61
  case study 61
  definition 60
  exercises 61
  key points 61
Cameron-Bandler, Leslie 168
change involvement 106
changing learner states 120–22
  exercises 121
  key points 121
  techniques 121
checklists 215–16
Chomsky, Naomi 168
chunking 185–6
coach style 12, 13
communicating clearly and effectively
  97–8
communication, emotional impact
  113
congruence 62
  examples of 62
  exercises 62
  key points 62
content clues 51–3
  case study 53
  key points 53
content reframes 82–3
context clues 51–3
  case study 53
  key points 53
context reframes 82
converger 11, 134, 135
Covey, Stephen 3, 158
creating rapport, *see* rapport creation
criticism 139
cross-over matching 19, 108

day dreaming 74
Dean, Ozzie 123
deletion 68, 74, 168
Dilts, Robert 87, 115, 127, 153
director style 12–13
displaced referential index 80
distortion 69, 74, 168
diverger 11, 134, 135
downtime 74

Ebbinghaus, Hermann 196
edits 205–7
  case study 207
  exercises 206–7
  key points 207
effective endings 216–17
elicitation metaphor 80
embedded commands 23, 91–3
  case study 92
  exercises 92
  key points 92
emotional engagement 25–6
  case study 27
  exercises 26
  key points 27
energy creation
  exercises 29
  key points 29
energy levels 27
environment creation 11–30
Ericson, Milton 2, 73
exercise bursts 27–9
  examples 28
  exercises 29
  key points 29
expectations, *see* high expectations
eye accessing cues 100–101

fatigue 27
feedback 138–46
  case study 146
  effective 140
  exercises 145
  how to give 144–5
  ineffective 140
  key points 145–6
  negative 139, 142–4
  positive 139, 140–42
  sandwich approach 138
  vs constructive criticism or advice
    giving 139
flexibility 5, 12, 30, 105
  developing 135
  personal 36–8
4 MAT system 133–4
functionalist style 14
future pacing 166–7

Gardner, Howard 158

generalization   69–70, 74, 168
goal review sheets   106
goal setting   105–7
   case study   107
   exercises   107
   key points   107
   model   106
   requirements   106
Grinder, John   2, 3, 68, 70, 205
Grinder, Michael   14
group dynamics creation   117–20
   exercises   120
   key points   120
   techniques   118–20
guided fantasy technique   74
gustatory predicates   71

high energy materials   21
high expectations
   creating and maintaining   21–5
   exercises   24
   key points   25
   key steps to creating   21–4
humanist   12, 14
humour   22, 122–5
   exercises   124
   guidelines for effective use   124
   key points   124–5
   key skills   123

identity, awareness   127–9
information gathering   94–7
   exercises   96
   key points   97
instruction   152–3
intelligences, seven   158–60
internal dialogue   209–10
interpreter style   12, 13
invisibles, awareness   127–9
involvement, maintaining   151–2
isomorphic metaphor   80

James, Tad   156, 164
Jensen, Eric   52, 75, 114, 118, 149
Jung, Carl   168

key events   26
kinesthetic metaphors   78–9
kinesthetic predicates   71

kinesthetic style   15
Kostere, Kim   80

language matching   71–2, 76
language patterns   18, 67–77
   altering states and meanings   72, 76
   belief systems revealed by   74–6
   case study   77
   exercises   76
   key points   76–7
language varieties   23
leading   108–12
   case study   110
   exercises   111–12
   key points   112
learner states, changing   120–22
learner styles   29–30
   exercises   30
   key points   30
learning, confirming   213–18
Learning Brain, The   52, 75
learning capacity   28
learning for next time   218
learning patterns
   case study   133
   creation   132–6
   exercises   136
   key points   136
learning process
   dietary effects   159
   use of baroque music   159
learning style preferences   12
Learning Styles Inventory   11, 29, 132
Learning Styles Questionnaire (LSQ)
   11, 29, 132–3
left brain
   functions   57
   jobs based on   59
levels of understanding   23
listener style   12
logical levels model   127, 130, 153
Lozanov, Georgi   155–6

McCarthy, Bernice   133
Malatesta, Linda   80
Maps, Models and the Structure of Reality
   80
Master Teaching Techniques   38
matching   18–19

Mehrabian, Albert   113
memory capacity   28
memory pegs   200–201
memory techniques   194–204
  blockages   199
  exercises   203
  key points   203–4
  key techniques   198
  long-term memory   199
  remembering names and faces   201
  research and findings   196–8
  short-term memory   199
  specific techniques   200–203
mental visualization   34, 200
Meta Model   68, 70–74, 76, 77, 99, 138
Meta position   49
Meta Programs   6, 42, 97, 151, 153, 168–83, 217
  basis of   169
  case study   172, 183–4
  current developments   181
  early work   168
  exercises   182
  general/specific   175–6
  internal/external   176–8
  key points   182–3
  moving toward/moving away   169–71
  possibility/necessity   171–2
  self/other   172–4
  similarity/difference   174–5
  time   180
  types   169
  uses   181–2
  where people place their interest   178–80
metaphors   77–82
  auditory   78
  exercises   81
  in memory techniques   202–3
  isomorphic   80
  key points   82
  key steps in building   79
  kinesthetic   78–9
  most useful types   79–80
  visual   78
methaphors, elicitation   80
Miller, George   168
mindmapping

benefits   59
guidelines   59
mnemonics   202

Neuro Linguistic Programming, *see* NLP
new behaviour generator   208–9
Nightingale Conant Accelerated Learning package   157, 158
NLP
  and training   6–7
  applications in the field of training   6–7
  background   2–7
  co-developers   2
  in accelerated learning   160
  processes involved   3
  specific applications in training programmes   7
non-sensory based words   71
non-verbal communication   97, 112–17
  case study   117
  exercises   116
  implications for trainer   113
  key points   116
  learner's   113–14
  specific exercise   115
  techniques   114–15
  trainer's   114

objectives, revising   213–14
O'Connor, Joseph   43
olfactory predicates   71
open environment   22
operating principles   3–5, 98
Ostrander, Nancy   159
Ostrander, Sheila   159
outcomes   21, 22, 24
  model   106
  process   213
  see also setting own personal outcomes

pacing   108–12
  and communication   109
  case study   110
  exercises   111–12
  key points   112

process 108
Palmer, Jerry 122
perceptual positions 48–50
  case study 50
  exercises 50
  first position 49
  key points 50
  second position 49
Perls, Fritz 2
personal development 49
personal flexibility 36–7
  exercises 37
  key points 38
physiology, key actions 17
positive beliefs 153
positive language 97
positive personal state 33–5
  case study 36
  exercises 34
  key points 36
positive start, key aspects 16
post-course self-evaluation 217
posture, key actions 17
pragmatist 11, 29, 133
predicates 71
  auditory 71
  gustatory 71
  kinesthetic 71
  olfactory 71
  visual 71
pre-exposure to topics 23
present state desired state 204–5
pre-suppositions 98–9

questions 99–100
quotes 90–91
  exercises 90
  key points 91

rapport creation 15–20, 108
  case study 17
  exercises 20
  key points 20
  key skills 16–20
  recognizing 19
rating 149
reference experiences 129–31
  case study 132
  exercises 131

key areas 130
key points 131
library of 130–31
reflector 11, 29, 133
reframing 82–4
  case study 84
  definition 82
  exercises 83–4
  key points 84
  main types 82
relevancy challenges 93–4
  case study 94
  examples 93
  exercises 93
  key points 94
representation systems 5, 41, 157
responding to questions and
  statements 68–71
reverse tests 148–50
  case study 150
  exercises 150
  key points 150
right brain
  functions 57
  jobs based on 59
Righting the Educational Conveyor Belt
  14
rituals 26
  case study 27
  examples 26
  exercises 26
  key points 27
Rose, Colin 157

Satir, Virginia 2
Schroeder, Lynn 159
self-awareness 49
senses 5
sensory acuity 28
setting own personal outcomes 44–5
  exercises 45
  key points 45
Seven Habits of Highly Effective People
  158
Seymour, John 43
significant events 23, 129–30
sleight of mouth 87–90
  case study 90
  definitions 87–8

exercises 89
key points 89
typical learner comment and trainer
    response 88–9
SMART criteria 164
Spitzer, R L 196
strategies 41–3
strategy elicitation 42–3
structuralist style 14
sub-modalities 40, 186–94
    action steps 189–90
    auditory 187
    basic steps for establishing 188
    case study 189
    exercises 191–3, 193
    general observations 191
    in memory techniques 202
    key points 186, 194
    kinesthetic 187–8
    visual 186–7
Super-Learning 2000 159
Super-teaching 114
SWISH 191–2
switching roles and styles 125–6
systemic belief approach 128–9

Taking Humour Seriously 122
tasking people 184–5
teaching process 39–40
    exercises 40
    key points 40
theorist 11, 29, 133
timelines 162–6

case study 165
exercises 166
finding 162
in therapy 164
key points 166
SMART criteria 164
Tracy, Brian 157
Trainer Type Inventory 12
training
    and NLP 6–7
    materials 22
    styles 11–15
    using a variety of techniques 51
Training Style Inventory 13
Training with NLP 43
transderivational search 80

ultradian rhythms 27
understanding, levels of 23
unsticking people 146–8
    exercises 148
    key points 148

values, awareness 127–9
visual aids 55
visual metaphors 78
visual predicates 71
visual style 14
visualizing 34, 200
voice tonalities 17–18, 33

Woodsmall, Wyatt 156, 196, 199